# Study Guide to Accompany
# TECHNICAL ANALYSIS

# Study Guide to Accompany
# TECHNICAL ANALYSIS

## Schwager on Futures

Thomas A. Bierovic
Steven C. Turner
Jack D. Schwager

**WILEY**

John Wiley & Sons, Inc.
New York • Chichester • Weinheim • Brisbane • Singapore • Toronto

ISBN: 0-471-12354-4

10 9 8 7 6 5 4 3 2 1

# Contents

# Preface

This study guide is a supplemental tool written for readers of *Schwager on Futures: Technical Analysis*. The accuracy of the reader's responses to the study-guide questions will be a barometer of how well he or she has understood the material. It should be apparent that this study guide is not a substitute for the complete text; rather, it complements and reinforces the Schwager material. The authors hope that this study guide will make *Schwager on Futures: Technical Analysis* an even more valuable trading companion, and that the reader's new knowledge will lead to many years of profitable futures trading.

The format of this study guide closely parallels *Schwager on Futures: Technical Analysis*, with questions for each chapter. Some of the chatpers also include problems to be solved. Solutions to the problems can be found by referring to the corresponding figure number in the text, *Technical Analysis*.

Questions and problems are found in Part One of this workbook and the answers and solutions in Part Two.

Thomas A. Bierovic
Dr. Steven C. Turner
Jack Schwager

# Study Guide to Accompany
# TECHNICAL ANALYSIS

# PART ONE

# Questions & Problems

# 1
# Charts: Forecasting Tool or Folklore

Price charts can be viewed as a picture that summarizes the net impact of all fundamental and psychological factors on a particular market for a specific time period. Chart analysis is a convenient and efficient method for learning about markets, although using charts as an indicator for future price direction has its advantages and disadvantages. Some of the advantages include providing an objective, concise price and volatility history, assisting in explaining historical market behavior, and providing a disciplinary tool for timing trades. Some disadvantages include its artistic rather than scientific character, subjective applications that are often difficult to quantify and duplicate, and the selection of a time frame within which a specific chart analysis is appropriate.

# Questions - Multiple Choice

**1.** The argument between random walkers and chart analysts centers on the _____ of prices.

a. explanatory factors

b. economic nature

c. statistical nature

d. psychological nature

**2.** The goal of a chart analyst is to identify periods within a price series which exhibit _____.

a. uptrends

b. breakouts

c. chaos

d. patterns

**3.** A trader seeking profits would prefer to be in a _____ market.

a. random

b. nonrandom

c. reversing

d. high-priced

**4.** Developing and updating charts imposes the skill of _____ on a trader.

a. discipline

b. forecasting

c. money management

d. economics

**5.** Attempting to buy low and sell high has a much lower probability of success than _____.

a. buying on Monday and selling on Friday

b. buying on the open and selling on the close

c. trading with the trend
d. selling in December and buying in January

**6.** Random walkers believe all of the following except that
_____.
a. no one can devise a system to predict market prices
b. prices have no memory
c. charts can only tell you what happened in the past
d. charts reveal basic behavioral patterns that can be used to antici-pate major market trends

**7.** All of the following are principal potential benefits of using charts except _____.
a. charts provide a concise price history
b. charts provide a good sense of the market's volatility
c. charts accurately forecast every market swing
d. charts can be used as a tool for timing and money management

**8.** The July 1980 Silver chart could justifiably be used to demon-strate that _____.
a. all price action is random
b. markets seem to exhibit periods of nonrandom behavior
c. all known fundamental data has already been discounted by a market at any given moment
d. a consensus exists as to the precise mathematical definitions for all chart patterns

# 2
# Types of Charts

Among the various types of charts available to the technical analyst are bar charts, point and figure charts, and candlestick charts. Bar charts can be constructed for any time period (e.g. monthly, weekly, daily, and five-minutes) with price on the vertical axis and time on the horizontal axis. For each unit of time, trading activity is represented by a vertical line with a length equal to the difference between the highest and lowest price. Attached to the vertical line are a small, horizontal line on the left that represents the open and a similar line on the right that represents the close.

An important issue when using weekly and monthly bar charts is whether to use a series of nearby futures contracts (plotting a contract until its expiration, then plotting the subsequent contract until its expiration, and so on) or to use continuous futures (a series that links successive contracts in such a way that price gaps are eliminated at rollover points). The appropriate series depends on the intended purpose.

Point and figure charts view all trading as a single, continuous stream and therefore ignore time. A point and figure chart consists of columns of X's that represents upward price movement of a predetermined magnitude and columns of O's that represent specified downward price movement. Point and figure chartists must decide two important parameters for their charts: box size and reversal size.

Candlestick charts add dimension and color to the bar chart. A two-dimensional "real body" represents the range between the open and the close, while extensions beyond this range to the high and low are shown as thin lines called "shadows".

## Questions - Multiple Choice

1. A _____ price series could result in consistent false price movements at regular intervals on a weekly bar chart.
   a. continuous
   b. nearby futures
   c. cash
   d. spread

2. If box size equals five cents and price increases by 13 cents, then _____ are placed in a column.
   a. three X's
   b. three O's
   c. two X's
   d. two O's

3. The only chart that uses color to convey information is the _____ chart.
   a. candlestick
   b. point and figure
   c. weekly bar
   d. close only

## Questions - Matching

Items:

(a) daily bar chart, (b) point and figure chart, (c) box size, (d) reversal size, (e) candlestick chart, (f) real body, (g) shadows, (h) nearest futures chart, (i) continuous futures, (j) close-only

1. The _____ consists of alternating columns of X's and O's.

2. The _____ adds dimension and color to the bar chart.

3. Cash price series and spreads are examples of price series that are depicted in _____ formats.

4. In a candlestick chart, the high and low are represented by thin lines called _____.

5. The _____ approach to linking a contract series will precisely reflect price swings but will not match actual historical price levels.

6. In a candlestick chart, the _____ represents the range between the open and close.

7. The _____ of a point and figure chart represents the minimum magnitude of a price move necessary to begin a new column of X's or O's.

8. The _____ may reflect significant distortion due to the price gap between the expiring month and the subsequent contract.

9. The _____ is most useful for timing purposes while the weekly and monthly charts provide important perspective.

10. The _____ of a point and figure chart represents the magnitude of a price move necessary to add another X to an existing column of X's or another O to an existing column of O's.

# 3
# Trends

Trends can be identified through several charting methods, including trend lines, trend channels, Thomas DeMark's TD lines, internal trend lines, and moving averages. A conventional definition of an uptrend is a succession of higher highs and higher lows, while a downtrend is a succession of lower lows and lower highs. An uptrend line connects a series of higher lows; a downtrend line connects a series of lower highs. Trend channels are sets of parallel trend lines that enclose a trend. TD trend lines are based on exactly two points and are drawn from right to left, contrary to convention. Internal trend lines connect the majority of relative highs or lows, rather than the extreme highs or lows, so as to best approximate a best-fit line of relative highs and relative lows.

Moving averages smooth a price series and make trends more discernible. A simple N moving average is defined as the average close of the past N days, including the current day. The smoothing properties of moving averages are achieved at the expense of introducing lags in the data. Turning points in moving averages always lag the corresponding transitions in the raw price series. Moving averages perform well in trending markets but generate many false signals in choppy markets.

## Questions - Multiple Choice

**1.** The drawing of conventional trend lines is a highly _____ process.

a. scientific

b. objective

c. mathematical

d. arbitrary

**2.** Moving averages generate _____ signals in choppy, sideways markets.

a. profitable

b. sell

c. buy

d. false

**3.** _____ trend lines are drawn from right to left.

a. Conventional

b. TD

c. Moving average

d. Parallel

**4.** The penetration of a downtrend line is a potential _____ signal.

a. buy

b. sell

c. hold

d. bearish

**5.** For a TD trend line, an N value of _____ will result in the most trend lines.

a. three

b. one

c. ten

d. five

**6.** The True High, which Schwager prefers for defining a relative high is _____.

a. the high or the previous close, whichever is higher

b. the high minus the low

c. the high plus the low

d. the high or the previous high, whichever is higher

**7.** Rallies approaching a downtrend line are often a good opportunity to initiate a _____ position.

a. long

b. spread

c. short

d. straddle

**8.** A _____ moving average is a result of today's close being higher than the close N plus 1 days ago.

a. rising

b. declining

c. TD

d. bearish

**9.** Schwager prefers _____ N values for TD trend lines, while DeMark prefers _____ N values.

a. smaller, larger

b. internal, external

c. fixed, fluctuating

d. larger, smaller

**10.** A(n) _____ line approximates the majority of relative lows.

a. TD uptrend

b. TD downtrend

c. internal uptrend

d. internal downtrend

## Problems

*NOTE: The figure numbers in parentheses are the corresponding text figures that can be referenced to check answers.*

**1.** Draw a conventional uptrend line beginning at point A.

Figure 3.4

UPTREND LINE: JULY 1993 SILVER

**2.** Draw a conventional downtrend line beginning at point A.

Figure 3.7

DOWNTREND LINE: COCOA NEAREST FUTURES

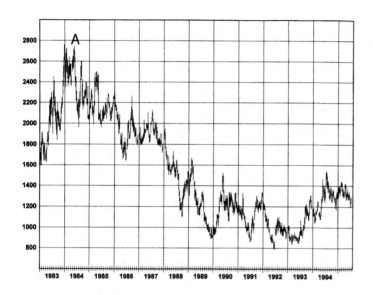

**3.** Draw an uptrend channel line.

Figure 3.9

UPTREND CHANNEL: JUNE 1991 EURODOLLAR

**4.** Draw a downtrend channel line.

Figure 3.10

DOWNTREND CHANNEL: SEPTEMBER 1992 COCOA

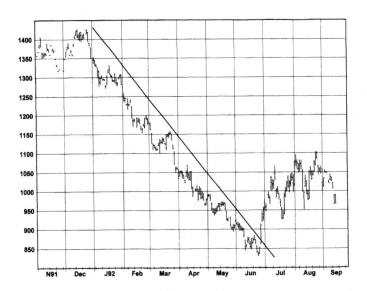

**5.** Redefine (redraw) the uptrend line after the trend line break at point A.

Figure 3.11

UPTREND LINE REDEFINED: JULY 1993 SILVER

**6.** Redefine (redraw) the downtrend line after the break at point A.

Figure 3.13

DOWNTREND LINE REDEFINED: MATIF NOTIONAL BOND CONTINU-
OUS FUTURES

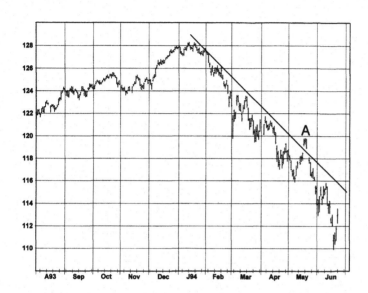

**7.** Draw the most recent TD downtrend line, using N = 3.

Figure 3.15

TD DOWNTREND LINE (N = 3): JULY 1995 SOYBEANS

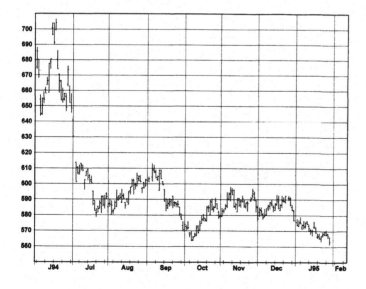

**8.** Draw the most recent TD uptrend line, using N = 8.

Figure 3.16

TD UPTREND LINE (N = 8): DECEMBER 1994 SWISS FRANC

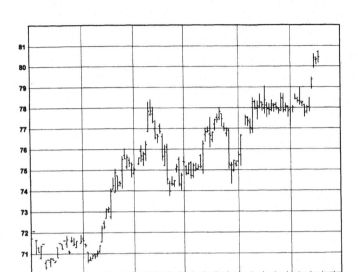

**9.** Draw the internal trend line beginning at point A.

Figure 3.26

INTERNAL TREND LINE VERSUS CONVENTIONAL TREND LINE: MARCH 1991 COTTON

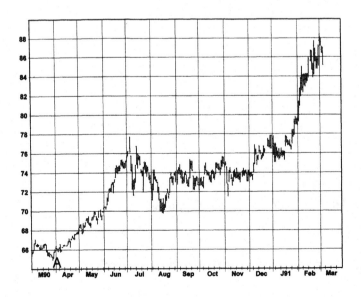

**10.** Draw the internal trend line beginning at point A.  Figure 3.34

INTERNAL TREND LINE VERSUS CONVENTIONAL TREND LINE:
SOYBEAN MEAL CONTINUOUS FUTURES

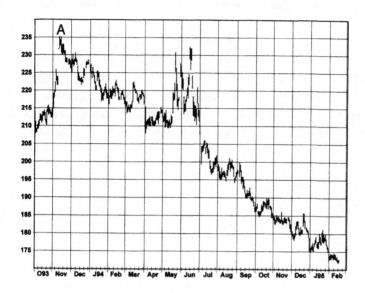

# 4
# Trading Ranges

Markets generally spend most of their time in trading ranges—horizontal corridors of price fluctuations. The upper and lower boundaries of trading ranges tend to define areas of support and resistance. Trading ranges are easily identifiable for the past but are nearly impossible to predict. Although it is difficult to trade profitably within trading ranges, breakouts from them often suggest a price move in the direction of the breakout.

## Questions - Multiple Choice

**1.** A breakout caused by a cluster of stop orders just above a resistance area will usually generate a _____.

a. trend
b. false signal
c. valid signal
d. false trend

**2.** The _____ the duration of a trading range the more potential for large price movement after a breakout.

a. shorter
b. narrower
c. longer
d. stronger

**3.** Breakouts from _____ trading ranges tend to provide _____ reliable trading signals.

a. longer, less
b. shorter, more
c. narrow, less
d. narrow, more

**4.** The increased use of technical analysis appears to have increased the frequency of _____.

a. trends
b. false signals
c. valid signals
d. false trends

**5.** The reliability of a breakout from a trading range is significantly improved by all of the following except _____.

a. price still beyond the range after a given number of days
b. a minimum percentage penetration

c. the number of thrust days

d. a lack of solid fundamental reasons to sustain the trend

**Problems**

*NOTE: The figure numbers in parentheses are the corresponding text figures that can be referenced to check answers.*

**1.** Identify the trading range by drawing horizontal lines across its upper and lower extremes.

Figure 4.5

UPSIDE BREAKOUT FROM TRADING RANGE: DECEMBER 1993 T-BOND

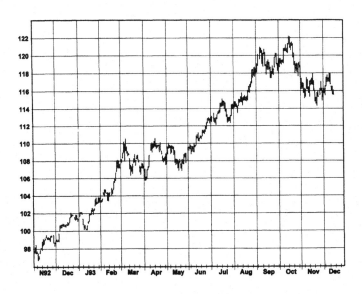

**2.** Identify the extended trading range by drawing horizontal lines across its upper and lower extremes.

Figure 4.7

UPSIDE BREAKOUT FROM EXTENDED TRADING RANGE: COPPER NEAREST FUTURES

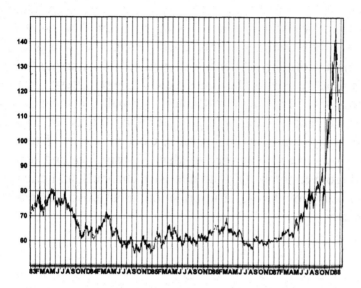

**3.** Identify two narrow trading ranges by drawing horizontal lines across the upper and lower extremes and circle the two break outs.

Figure 4.9

UPSIDE BREAKOUTS FROM NARROW TRADING RANGES: SEPTEMBER 1990 BRITISH POUND

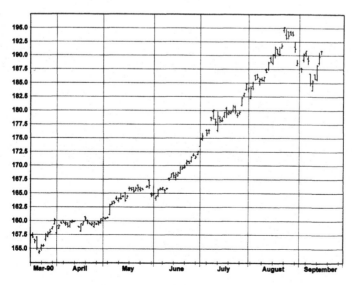

# 5
# Support and Resistance

Prices tend to meet resistance at the upper end of well-established trading ranges and to find support at the lower end. Although some traders attempt to sell rallies and to buy declines within trading ranges, it is a difficult strategy to implement profitably. After a sustained bullish breakout from a trading range, the old resistance becomes new support; after a bearish breakout, old support becomes new resistance. Normally, resistance will be encountered in the general vicinity of previous major highs and support in the general vicinity of previous major lows. Concentrations of relative highs and relative lows can also be used to identify resistance and support areas. Trend lines (conventional, TD, and internal), channels, and price envelope bands can also provide useful information about possible areas of support and resistance.

## Questions - Multiple Choice

**1.** After a sustained penetration of a prior low, that price level be-comes an area of _____.

a.  support

b.  resistance

c.  concentration

d.  a price envelope

**2.** As a technical trader, you would be most confident of a buy sig-nal after a sustained breakout from a resistance level of a _____ duration.

a.  one-month

b.  three-month

c.  one-year

d.  three-year

**3.** The approach of using concentrations of previous relative highs and lows to define support and resistance can generally not be applied to _____ futures charts.

a.  daily individual

b.  daily continuous

c.  weekly

d.  monthly

**4.** _____ are used to develop price envelope bands.

a.  Trend lines

b.  Trend channels

c.  Moving averages

d.  Internal trend lines

**5.** A five percent price envelope band with a current moving aver-age of 200 would have an upper band of _____ and a low er band of _____.

a.  210, 190

b.  205, 195

c.    300, 100

d.    support, resistance

## Problems

*NOTE: The figure numbers in parentheses are the corresponding text figures that can be referenced to check answers.*

**1.**   Identify the trading range by drawing horizontal lines across its high and low extremes. Then circle both the breakout from the trading range and the test of the line of old resistance/new support.

Figure 5.2

SUPPORT NEAR TOP OF PRIOR TRADING RANGE: DECEMBER 1993 SOYBEAN OIL

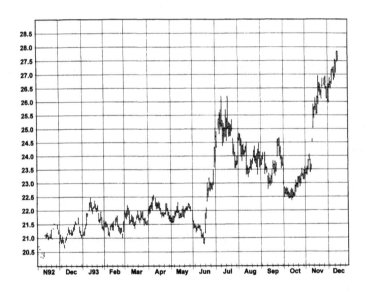

**2.** Circle the test of the line of old support/new resistance.

Figure 5.3

RESISTANCE NEAR BOTTOM OF PRIOR TRADING RANGE: DECEMBER 1992 CANADIAN DOLLAR

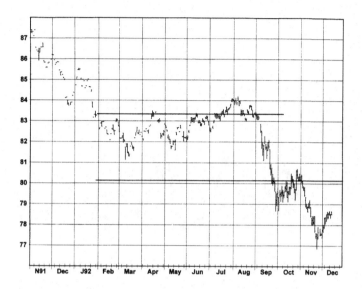

**3.** Identify the support zone by drawing horizontal lines across concentrations of prior relative lows and highs.

Figure 5.15

SUPPORT ZONE DEFINED BY CONCENTRATION OF PRIOR RELATIVE LOWS AND HIGHS: SWISS FRANC NEAREST FUTURES

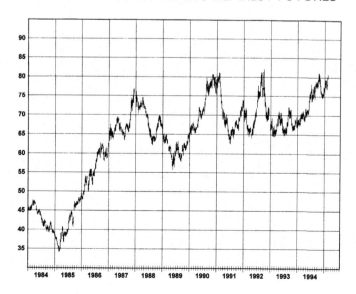

**4.** Identify the resistance zone by drawing horizontal lines across concentrations of prior relative highs and lows.

Figure 5.22

RESISTANCE ZONE DEFINED BY CONCENTRATION OF PRIOR RELATIVE HIGHS AND LOWS: DEUTSCHE MARK CONTINUOUS FUTURES

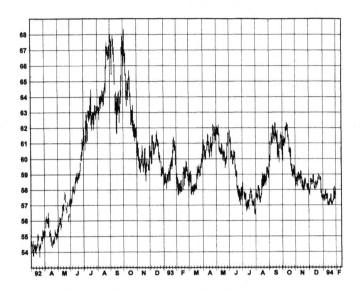

# 6
# Chart Patterns

Chart patterns can be divided into three major categories: one-day patterns, continuation patterns, and top-and-bottom formations. One-day patterns include gap, spike, reversal, thrust, run, and wide-ranging days. Continuation patterns are various types of congestion phases that form within long-term trends. A continuation pattern is generally expected to be resolved by a price swing in the same direction that preceded its formation. Common continuation patterns include triangles (symmetrical, ascending, and descending), flags, and pennants. Chart patterns that often indicate market turning points are V tops and bottoms, double tops and bottoms, head and shoulders tops and bottoms, rounded tops and bottoms, triangles, wedges, and island reversals.

## Questions - Multiple Choice

**1.** A gap day's low is above the previous day's _____, or the high is below the previous day's _____.

a. high, low

b. low, high

c. open, close

d. spike, thrust

**2.** A(n) _____ gap occurs within a trading range and is not particularly significant.

a. common

b. breakaway

c. runaway

d. exhaustion

**3.** In very powerful bull and bear markets, a series of _____ gaps can occur on consecutive days.

a. common

b. breakaway

c. runaway

d. exhaustion

**4.** A(n) _____ gap occurs after an extended price move and is soon followed by a trend reversal.

a. common

b. breakaway

c. runaway

d. exhaustion

**5.** A(n) _____ gap occurs when prices surge beyond the extreme of a trading range, leaving an area in which no trading activity has taken place.

a. common

b. breakaway

c. runaway

d. exhaustion

**6.** The significance of a spike high will be enhanced by all of the following except _____.

a. a wide difference between the spike high and the highs of the preceding and succeeding days

b. a close near the low of the day's range

c. a close near the high of the day's range

d. a substantive price advance preceding the spike's formation

**7.** Schwager suggests defining a reversal low day as a day that witnesses a new low in a down move but then reverses to close above the previous day's _____.

a. high

b. low

c. open

d. close

**8.** During bull markets, _____ days significantly outnumber _____ days.

a. reversal, run

b. downthrust, upthrust

c. upthrust, downthrust

d. down run days, up run days

**9.** A wide-ranging day with a weak close that occurs after a major advance can often signal _____.

a. a continuation pattern

b. support

c. an upside trend reversal

d. a downside trend reversal

**10.** All of the following are types of continuation patterns except
_____.

a.  V tops and bottoms
b.  flags
c.  pennants
d.  symmetrical triangles

**11.** Narrow-band, short-duration congestion phases within trends include _____.

a.  head and shoulders tops and bottoms
b.  flags and pennants
c.  ascending triangles
d.  runaway gaps

**12.** Which of the following is not one of the three basic types of triangle patterns?

a.  parallel
b.  symmetrical
c.  ascending
d.  descending

**13.** A flag or pennant that forms near the bottom of a trading range is a _____ signal.

a.  trend-reversal
b.  bullish
c.  bearish
d.  false

**14.** A head and shoulders is considered complete only after _____.

a.  the neckline is formed
b.  the second shoulder is formed
c.  the neckline is penetrated
d.  the distance between the neckline and head can be determined

**15.** A(n) _____ is formed when prices gap higher after an extended advance, trade one or more days leaving the gap open, and then gap lower.

a.   rounded bottom

b.   island bottom

c.   saucer top

d.   island top


## Questions - Matching

Items:

(a) gap day, (b) spike low, (c) reversal low day, (d) upthrust day, (e) down run day, (f) wide-range day, (g) symmetrical triangle, (h) ascending triangle, (i) descending triangle, (j) V top, (k) double bottom, (l) head-and-shoulders top, (m) rounded bottom, (n) rising wedge, (o) island top reversal

**1.**   A consolidation pattern with a falling top line and a flat bottom line. _____

**2.**   A strongly trending day with a true low below the lowest true low of the past N days and a true high greater than the highest true high of the subsequent N days. _____

**3.**   A reversal pattern that is completed by a price move above the reaction high between two lows that were formed in the same general price vicinity. _____

**4.**   A day in which the low is above the previous day's high or the high is below the previous day's low. _____

**5.**   A turn-on-a-dime reversal pattern after an extended upmove.

_____

**6.**   A day that witnesses a new low in a decline and then reverses to close above the previous day's close or high. _____

7.  A formation (usually a continuation pattern) identified by trend lines that converge at the same (or approximately the same) angles. _____

8.  A three-point formation in which the middle high is above the high points on either side. _____

9.  A day whose low is sharply below the low of the preceding and succeeding days. _____

10. A pattern occurring when prices gap higher after an extended advance, trade one or more days leaving the gap open, and then gap lower. _____

11. A reversal pattern with an outer perimeter conforming to a saucer shape. _____

12. A day whose volatility significantly exceeds the average volatility of recent trading days. _____

13. A pattern in which prices edge steadily higher with prices unable to accelerate on the upside despite probes into new high ground. _____

14. A day that closes above the previous day's high. _____

15. A formation (usually a continuation pattern) identified by a flat upper line and a rising lower line. _____

## Problems

*NOTE: The figure numbers in parentheses are the corresponding text figures that can be referenced to check answers.*

**1.** Identify the types of gaps at points A, B, and C.

Figure 6.2

PRICE GAPS: FEBRUARY 1995 HOGS

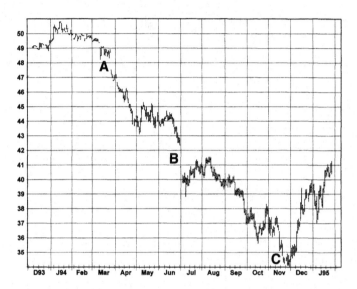

**2.** Draw the symmetrical triangle.

Figure 6.20

SYMMETRICAL TRIANGLE: FCOJ CONTINUOUS FUTURES

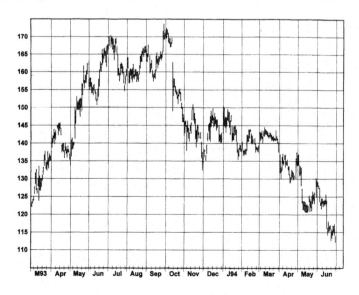

**3.** Draw the ascending triangle.

Figure 6.23

ASCENDING TRIANGLE: OCTOBER 1992 SUGAR

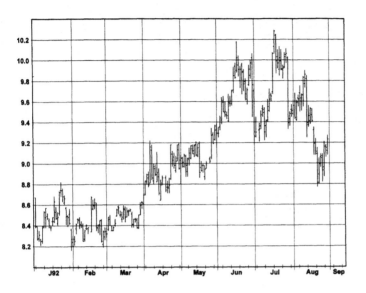

**4.** Draw the descending triangle.

Figure 6.24

DESCENDING TRIANGLE: SOYBEAN OIL CONTINUOUS FUTURES

**5.** Draw six flags and four pennants.

Figure 6.28

FLAGS AND PENNANTS: JULY 1992 COCOA

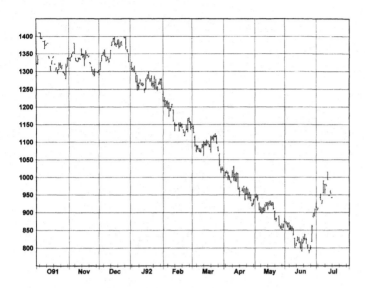

**6.** Draw horizontal lines at the high and low extremes of the extended trading range and draw the pennant above the top of the trading range.

Figure 6.31

PENNANT ABOVE TOP OF TRADING RANGE AS BULLISH SIGNAL: JULY 1993 SOYBEANS

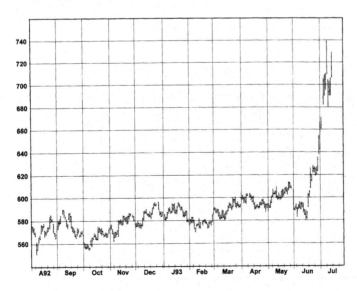

**7.** Draw horizontal lines at the high and low extremes of the trading range and draw the flag that appears near the bottom of the trading range.

Figure 6.35

FLAG NEAR BOTTOM OF TRADING RANGE AS BEARISH SIGNAL: JUNE 1994 EURODOLLAR

**8.** Circle the two highs that form the double top and the low that must be penetrated to confirm the double top.

Figure 6.40
DOUBLE TOP: AUSTRALIAN 10-YEAR BOND WEEKLY CONTINUOUS FUTURES

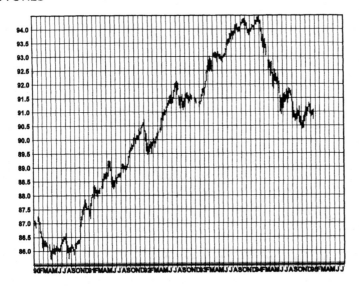

**9.** Circle the two lows that form the double bottom and the high that must be penetrated to confirm the double bottom.

Figure 6.41

DOUBLE BOTTOM: UNLEADED GAS CONTINUOUS FUTURES

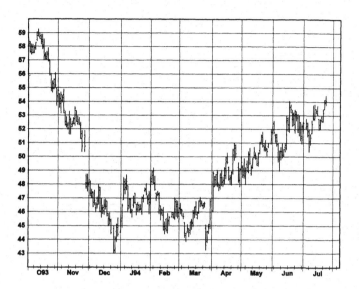

**10.** Label the left shoulder, head, right shoulder, and neckline of this head-and-shoulders top.

Figure 6.46

HEAD-AND-SHOULDERS TOP: JUNE 1991 CRUDE OIL

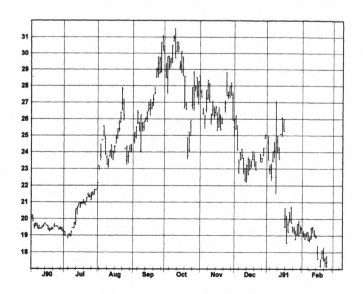

**11.** Label the left shoulder, head, right shoulder, and neckline of this head-and-shoulders bottom.

Figure 6.47
HEAD-AND-SHOULDERS BOTTOM: DECEMBER 1992 COFFEE

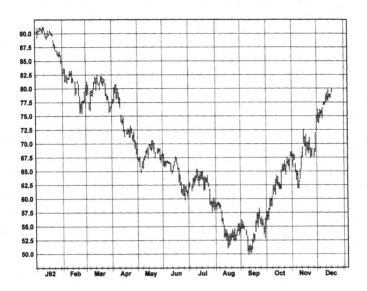

**12.** Draw the primary and secondary rounding tops.

Figure 6.50
TWO ROUNDING TOPS: MAY 1995 WHEAT

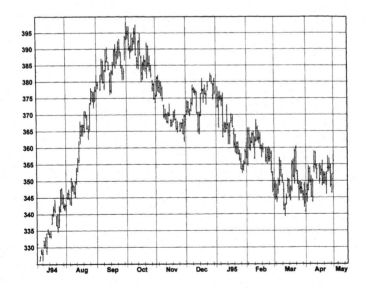

38

**13.** Draw the rounding bottom.
Figure 6.53
ROUNDING BOTTOM: AUGUST 1992 NATURAL GAS

**14.** Draw the declining wedge.
Figure 6.59
MULTIYEAR DECLINING WEDGE: GOLD WEEKLY NEAREST FUTURES

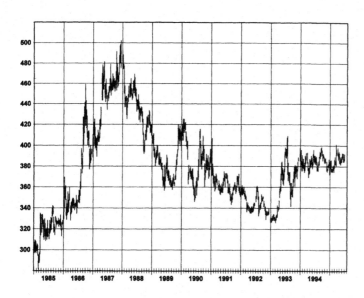

**15.** Circle the island top.    Figure 6.63

ISLAND TOP: JANUARY 1994 PLATINUM

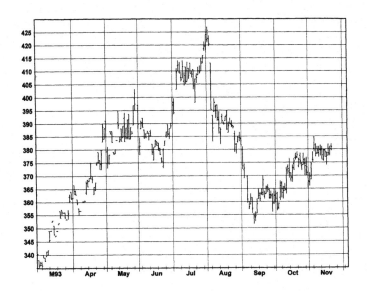

# 7
# Is Chart Analysis Still Valid?

Chart analysis is a highly individualized endeavor, with success or failure critically dependent on the trader's skill and experience. Although a simplistic, mechanical response to chart signals will probably not lead to trading success, a more sophisticated use of charts can provide the core of an effective trading plan. A disciplined adherence to the principles of money management that strictly limits losses and allows profits to run is essential in the successful application of chart analysis to trading. Chart analysis can also be made more effective by requiring confirmation conditions such as time delays, minimum percent penetrations, and specific chart patterns before a chart-based entry signal is acted upon. Another attribute of a successful chart trader is the ability to synthesize the various components of the overall picture rather than just recognizing and interpreting individual patterns. The chart analyst who is also a competent fundamental analyst has an advantage over the trader who bases their decisions solely on chart patterns. Finally, recognizing and acting upon a market's failure to follow through in the direction of a key chart signal can greatly enhance the effectiveness of the chartist's approach.

## Questions - Multiple Choice

**1.** Disciplined money management demands that _____.

a.  losses are rigidly controlled and profitable trades are allowed to run their course

b.  confirmation signals should be ignored

c.  the number of winning trades far exceeds the number of losing trades

d.  fundamental information is ignored

**2.** In setting confirmation rules, a _____ exists between minimizing false signals and maximizing profits in winning trades.

a.  contradiction

b.  time delay

c.  tradeoff

d.  positive correlation

**3.** Waiting for two thrust days in the direction of a breakout from a trading range is an example of _____.

a.  a fundamental confirmation

b.  a minimum percent penetration

c.  a market failure

d.  a specific chart pattern

**4.** A rally above the right shoulder of a head-and-shoulders top after a decline below the neckline is an example of _____.

a.  a minimum percent penetration

b.  a time delay

c.  a failed signal

d.  a fundamental consideration

**5.** Chart analysis remains a valid trading tool despite its widespread usage due to _____ adaptation.

a. individualized

b. objective

c. corporate

d. mechanical

# 8
# Midtrend Entry and Pyramiding

The primary goals when entering a market in the midst of a major trend should be favorable timing and risk control. Four key strategies can be employed to help achieve these objectives: (1) percent retracement, (2) reversal of minor reaction, (3) continuation pattern and trading-range breakout, and (4) reaction to long-term moving average. Percent retracement attempts to capitalize on the natural tendency of a market to partially retrace prior price swings. A trader can initiate a position when the market retraces a given percentage (35 to 65%) of the price swing from the last relative low or relative high. The reversal-of-minor-reaction strategy enters a market after the resumption of a major trend following a minor reaction. Continuation patterns and trading-range breakouts, which were discussed in Chapter 6, can also serve as midtrend entry signals. Reactions to a long-term moving average can be interpreted as signals that the reaction to the main trend is near an end.

Pyramiding (adding to existing positions) calls for three additional guidelines: (1) additional positions should only be taken if the last position placed is currently profitable, (2) no additional positions should be taken if the intended stop point would generate a net loss for the entire position, and (3) pyramid units should be no greater than the base (initial) position size.

## Questions - Multiple Choice

**1.** A reasonable choice for the percentage retracement necessary for midtrend entry or pyramiding is _____.

a. 5 to 10%

b. 15 to 25%

c. 35 to 65%

d. 55 to 85%

**2.** A reaction count would typically be used in a _____ strategy.

a. percent-retracement

b. reversal-of-minor-reaction

c. continuation-pattern

d. reaction-to-long-term-moving-average

**3.** Entering the market in the middle of a flag is an example of a _____ strategy.

a. percent-retracement

b. reversal-of-minor-reaction

c. continuation-pattern

d. reaction-to-long-term-moving-average

**4.** Using a reaction to a moving average signal approach, which of the following would be a buy signal?

a. a 10-day moving average crossing a 40-day moving average from above

b. a daily price bar crossing a 40-day moving average from above

c. a 10-day moving average crossing a 40-day moving average from below

d. a daily price bar crossing a 40-day moving average from below

**5.** All of the following guidelines apply to pyramiding except, _____.

a. don't pyramid unless you can add the new contracts at a more favorable price (lower than the last addition if long, higher than the last addition if short)

b.  don't pyramid if the stop point would imply a net loss for the entire position

c.  don't pyramid unless the last unit placed is profitable

d.  don't add pyramid units greater than the size of the initial position

## Problems

*NOTE: The figure numbers in parentheses are the corresponding text figures that can be referenced to check answers.*

1.  Label the reaction days (1-4) and the thrust days (A-C) that represent the reversal-of-minor-reaction pattern in June and July. Circle the point at which you would buy the market based on the completion of this pattern and circle the point at which you would set your protective stop. Then label the reaction days (1-4) and the thrust days (A-C) that represent the reversal-of-minor-reaction pattern in September and October. Circle the point at which you would buy the market based on the completion of this pattern and circle the point at which you would set your protective stop.

Figure 8.4

REVERSAL OF MINOR REACTION (MARCH 1995 SUGAR)

**2.** Draw the four continuation patterns (one pennant and three flags) that form in October-December. Circle the days on which you would buy the market based on breakouts from these patterns. Draw a horizontal line for each of the four initial protective stops.

Figure 8.5
CONTINUATION PATTERN BREAKOUTS AS ENTRY SIGNALS (MARCH 1995 COTTON)

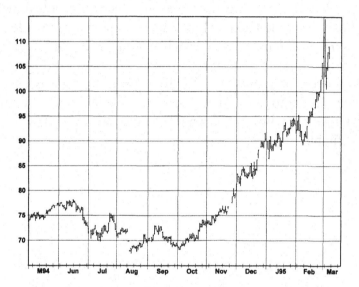

**3.** Circle the four days that set up possible buying opportunities based on a reaction below the long-term moving average.

Figure 8.6
REACTION TO LONG-TERM MOVING AVERAGE (SEPTEMBER 1994 DEUTSCHE MARK)

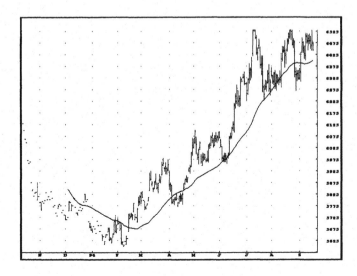

47

# 9
# Choosing Stop-Loss Points

Because successful trading is dependent on strictly controlling losses, a precise stop-loss point should be determined before entering a trade. The stop should be located at or before the point at which price movement would cause a transition in the technical picture. Stop points can be determined by using technical-reference points such as trend lines, trading ranges, flags and pennants, wide-ranging days, and relative highs and lows. If the risk implied by even the closest technically significant point is excessive, the trader may decide to use a money stop—a stop determined by the desired dollar-risk level. Trailing stops can be used to lock in gains when a trade becomes profitable.

## Questions - Multiple Choice

**1.** Placing stop-loss orders when entering a trade is part of
_____.

a. fundamental analysis
b. technical analysis
c. tax management
d. money management

**2.** In an uptrending market, a stop-loss order or a trailing stop can be placed _____ the trend line.

a. above
b. below
c. on
d. at the beginning of

**3.** If the nearest technically significant chart point is excessively far from the entry point of a trade, a _____ stop is frequently the best alternative.

a. cancel-if-close
b. market-order
c. money
d. breakout

**4.** A _____ can be used to protect profits.

a. cancel-if-close order
b. stop-loss order
c. stop-and-reverse strategy
d. trailing stop

**5.** Stops should be changed only in order to _____.

a. reduce risk or protect profits
b. give a market more room to move

c. prevent getting stopped out at the bottom of a move (the top if short)

d. possibly avoiding a losing trade

## Problems

*NOTE: The figure numbers in parentheses are the corresponding text figures that can be referenced to check answers.*

**1.** Draw two horizontal lines to identify the trading range from November to February. Circle the breakout from the trading range and label the maximum protective-stop point for the new short position.

Figure 9.1

STOP PLACEMENT FOLLOWING TRADING RANGE BREAKOUT: DECEMBER 1994 T-BOND

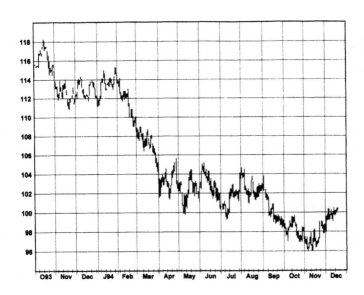

**2.** If you bought this market on a breakout in October above the September high, where would you place your protective stop? Circle two meaningful chart points.

Figure 9.4

STOP PLACEMENT AT RELATIVE LOWS: MARCH 1995 COTTON

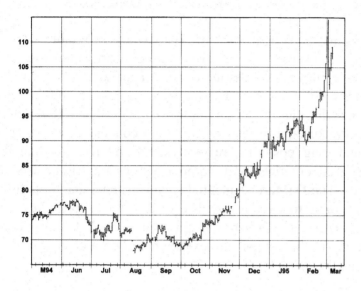

# 10
# Setting Objectives and Other Position Exit Criteria

This chapter presents several approaches for exiting profitable trades. Chart-based objectives utilize the repetitive nature of chart patterns to estimate potential price moves. A measured-move approach relies on the premise that markets will move in equal-size price swings. The rule of seven uses a common set of multipliers (dividing 7 by 5, 4, 3, and 2) to determine objectives. Support-and-resistance levels are convenient exit objectives for short and long positions, respectively. Similarly, overbought/oversold indicators reflect vulnerability to price actions and can be used to develop exit points. The DeMark sequential signals when a market is fully extended and vulnerable to a major trend reversal. Other approaches that can be used for determining when to exit positions include taking a contrary opinion, setting trailing stops, and exiting based on a change in personal opinion about the market.

## Questions - Multiple Choice

**1.** In general, a relative strength index (RSI) of 25 indicates a(n) _____ market.

a. neutral
b. oversold
c. overbought
d. bull

**2.** Conventional wisdom maintains that after a breakout from a head-and-shoulders formation, the market will move at least a distance equal to the distance from the _____.

a. beginning of one shoulder to the end of the other shoulder
b. top of the nearest shoulder to the neckline
c. inside of one shoulder to the outside of the other shoulder
d. top of the head to the neckline

**3.** The _____ stage in the DeMark sequential _____ condition requires nine or more consecutive closes that are lower than the corresponding closes four trading days earlier.

a. setup, sell
b. countdown, sell
c. setup, buy
d. countdown, buy

**4.** A(n) _____ approach to setting exit objectives assumes that market-price swings occur in approximately equal size.

a. rule-of-seven
b. DeMark-sequential
c. measured-move
d. overbought/oversold

**5.** The major difficulty with using a contrary-opinion approach to exiting trades is measuring market _____.

a. trends

b.   sentiment

c.   volatility

d.   overbought/oversold conditions

6.   Using a rule-of-seven approach to exiting a bull market that had
     an initial wave of 80 from a low of 525, the three exit points
     would be _____.

a.   637, 665, 711

b.   665, 711, 805

c.   637, 711, 805

d.   637, 665, 805

7.   The intersection stage in a DeMark sequential can only occur on
     or after the _____th day of the _____ stage.

a.   8, setup

b.   13, countdown

c.   9, setup

d.   9, countdown

8.   A resistance level would provide an exit objective in a
     _____ trade position.

a.   short

b.   spread

c.   straddle

d.   long

9.   The _____ approach to developing exit objectives is the
     most subjective.

a.   DeMark-sequential

b.   rule-of-seven

c.   chart-based

d.   overbought/oversold

**10.** A _____ approach attempts to permit a profitable trade to run its course, but a trader will never sell the high or buy the low with this method.

a. trailing-stop

b. contrary-opinion

c. measured-move

d. rule-of-seven

## Problems

*NOTE: The figure numbers in parentheses are the corresponding text figures that can be referenced to check answers.*

**1.** Given the price swing from point A to point B, draw a horizontal line to mark the measured-move objective for the upswing that began at point C.

Figure 10.2

MEASURED MOVE: WHEAT CONTINUOUS FUTURES

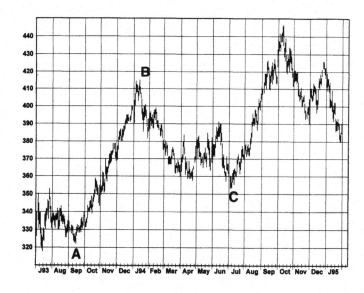

**2.** Label the nine periods of the setup (1-9) and the 13 periods of the countdown (1-13) for the DeMark Sequential on this monthly gold chart.

Figure 10.16

DEMARK SEQUENTIAL: GOLD MONTHLY NEAREST FUTURES

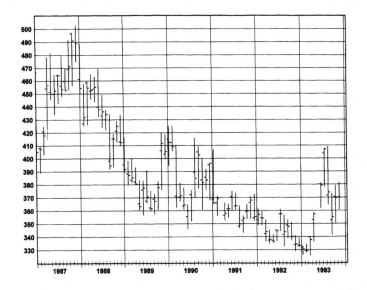

# 11

# The Most Important Rule in Chart Analysis

A failed chart signal is a reliable indicator that suggests a significant move in the opposite direction. Types of failed signals include bull and bear traps, false trend-line breakouts, filled gaps, returns to spike and wide-ranging day extremes, counter-to-anticipated breakouts from flags or pennants, opposite-direction breakouts from flags or pennants following normal breakouts, penetrations of tops and bottoms, and breaking of curvature. The discipline and flexibility required to exit a trade at a loss and to immediately reverse the position when market behavior warrants are essential to the effective synthesis of chart analysis and trading.

## Questions - Multiple Choice

1.  When a bear trap is recognized, one should take a _____ position.

a.  short

b.  spread

c.  straddle

d.  long

2.  After the penetration of a spike high, a close _____ the spike's _____ would be an example of a failed signal.

a.  below, low

b.  above, high

c.  at, high

d.  at, close

3.  A novice trader will _____ a failed signal while a highly skilled trader will _____ a failed signal.

a.  exit on, ignore

b.  ignore, profit from

c.  ignore, exit on

d.  profit from, exit on

4.  Using filled gaps as a failed signal is enhanced if the filled gap is a _____ gap.

a.  common

b.  breakaway

c.  runaway

d.  exhaustion

5.  According to Schwager, _____ trend-line breakout signals are more reliable than _____ trend-line breakout signals.

a.  bearish, bullish

b.  bullish, bearish

c.   conventional, false

d.   false, conventional

**6.**   A(n) _____ beyond the opposite end of a flag is required to confirm a failed signal.

a.   open

b.   high

c.   low

d.   close

**7.**   A _____ trap is among the most reliable indicators of a major _____.

a.   bull, bottom

b.   bull, top

c.   bear, downturn

d.   bear, top

**8.**   All of the following are recommended confirmation conditions for bull and bear traps except _____.

a.   overbought/oversold confirmation

b.   strong price confirmation

c.   time confirmation

d.   initial price confirmation

**9.**   A flag formation near a contract high is normally a _____ signal.

a.   failed

b.   bearish

c.   bullish

d.   reversal

**10.**   The _____ a technical signal becomes the more failed signals occur.

a.   more bullish

b. more bearish

c. less popular

d. more popular

## Problems

*NOTE: The figure numbers in parentheses are the corresponding text figures that can be referenced to check answers.*

**1.** Circle the bull trap in May.

Figure 11.1

BULL TRAP: OCTOBER 1993 SUGAR

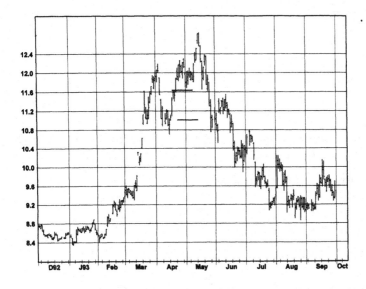

**2.** Circle the bear trap in February.

Figure 11.3

BEAR TRAP: JULY 1993 SILVER

**3.** Draw the conventional bearish trend line (January-June) and circle the false breakout.

Figure 11.7

FALSE BREAKOUT OF DOWNTREND LINE: DECEMBER 1994 OATS

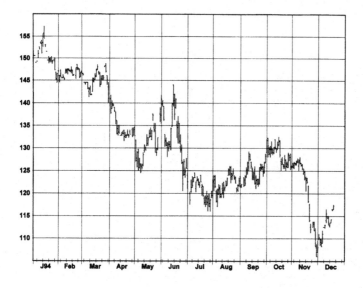

**4.** Circle the wide-ranging day in May that fills April's upside gap.

Figure 11.10

FILLED UPSIDE GAP: MARCH 1991 SUGAR

**5.** Circle the spike high in July and the penetration of the spike high in November.

Figure 11.16

PENETRATION OF SPIKE HIGH: MARCH 1994 SOYBEAN OIL

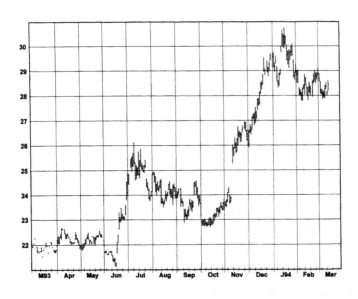

**6.** Draw the flag that forms in December and circle the counter-to-anticipated breakout.

Figure 11.28

COUNTER-TO-ANTICIPATED BREAKOUT OF FLAG PATTERN: MARCH 1992 COCOA

**7.** Draw the pennant that forms in June and circle the counter-to-anticipated breakout.

Figure 11.30

COUNTER-TO-ANTICIPATED BREAKOUT OF PENNANT: MARCH 1993 COTTON

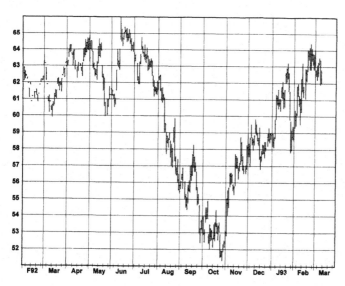

**8.** Circle the October confirmation of the head-and-shoulders top; then, circle the December confirmation of the failure of the head-and-shoulders top.

Figure 11.40

FAILED HEAD-AND-SHOULDERS TOP PATTERNS: JUNE 1993 T-BOND

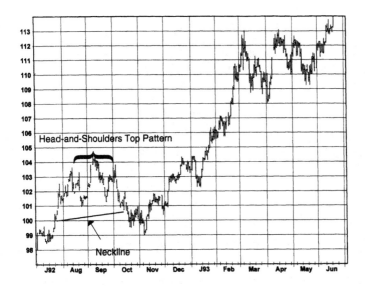

# 12

# Linking Contracts for Long-Term Chart Analysis: Nearest versus Continuous Futures

The application of chart analysis requires linking successive futures contracts into a single chart. Two common approaches, nearest futures and continuous futures, exist for creating linked contracts. A nearest-futures price series uses the nearest contract price until its expiration and then uses the next nearest contract price, and so on. A continuous-futures price series adjusts for the price spread between contracts when the switch is made. That is, at the rollover date, the new contract price is adjusted by the difference between the old and new contract prices. The procedure continues throughout the life of the chart. In addition, the scale of the entire price series is shifted by the cumulative adjustment factor to set the current price of the series equal to the price of the current contract. A nearest-futures series accurately reflects price levels, while a continuous-futures series reflects price swings. The continuous series will parallel the equity fluctuations of a continually held long position, whereas a nearest-futures series can be very misleading in this respect.

## Questions - Multiple Choice

**1.** The December corn contract expires at $2.84, and the next near-est contract (March) closes at $2.90.  On the next day, March corn closes at $2.95.  A nearest-futures chart would show a(n) _____ gain.

a.  5 cents

b.  1 cent

c.  11 cents

d.  6 cents

**2.** A nearest-futures chart accurately reflects price _____.

a.  moves

b.  levels

c.  swings

d.  volatility

**3.** Linked futures charts are especially useful for identifying _____.

a.  flags

b.  pennants

c.  major tops and bottoms

d.  volatility

**4.** A trader decides to use December and July cotton contracts to develop a continuous-futures chart.  December closes at 76 cents on the rollover date, and July closes at 85 cents.  On the next rollover date, July closes at 71 cents and December closes at 68 cents.  The next day, December closes at 69 cents, so the contin uous-futures contract price would be _____ cents (before making a scale adjustment).

a.  57

b.  58

c.  60

d.  63

**5.** For a more complete and more reliable longer-term analysis of a market's behavior, Schwager recommends using _____.

a. point-and-figure charts

b. a combination of nearest and continuous price series

c. nearest-futures charts

d. continuous-futures charts

# 13

# An Introduction to Japanese Candlestick Charts

Candle charts are Japan's oldest and most popular form of technical analysis. The broad part of the candlestick line—the "real body"—represents the range between the open and the close. If the real body is black (filled in), the close was lower than the open; if the real body is white (empty), the close was higher than the open. The thin lines above and below the real body are called the "shadows." The top of the upper shadow represents the high of the session, and the bottom of the lower shadow represents the low.

The color and shape of candlesticks provide visual insight into who is winning the battle between the bulls and the bears. A long, white real body demonstrates that the bulls are in charge, while a long, black real body tells us that the bears are in control. A small real body (whether white or black) indicates a period in which the bulls and bears are more in balance. Candles can be drawn for all time frames, from intraday to monthly charts.

Some of the most significant candlestick patterns include the doji, hammer, hanging man, shooting star, engulfing pattern, dark cloud cover, piercing line, morning and evening star, and windows. Although computerized tests of these patterns in isolation have not been encouraging, it is entirely possible that a more sophisticated analysis of candlestick charts—taking into account the context in which the individual patterns occur—could be very useful. Also, many traders prefer the alternative visual depiction of price data offered by Japanese candlestick charts.

## Questions - Multiple Choice

**1.** A black real body indicates a _____ market.
a. bearish
b. bullish
c. neutral
d. trending

**2.** A _____ is a three-day pattern which signals a bottom reversal.
a. shooting star
b. morning star
c. evening star
d. doji

**3.** A(n) _____ forms when the low of today's lower shadow is above the high of yesterday's upper shadow.
a. morning star
b. evening star
c. rising window
d. falling window

**4.** In candlestick charts, the most emphasis is placed on the _____.
a. upper shadow
b. lower shadow
c. close
d. real body

**5.** A falling window is usually a _____ pattern.
a. bullish-continuation
b. bearish-continuation
c. bullish-reversal
d. bearish-reversal

## Questions - Matching

Items:

(a) real body, (b) shadows, (c) doji, (d) hammer, (e) hanging man, (f) shooting star, (g) bullish engulfing pattern, (h) dark cloud cover, (i) evening star, (j) window

1. In an uptrend, a candlestick with a long upper shadow, little or no lower shadow, and a small real body near the low.
   _____

2. A major top-reversal pattern formed by three candlesticks.
   _____

3. The thick part of the candle, defined by the opening and closing prices. _____

4. In an uptrend, a small real body with little or no upper shadow and a very long lower shadow. _____

5. A gap. _____

6. In an uptrend, a long, white candlestick followed by a black candlestick that opens above the prior white candlestick's high and closes well into the white candlestick's real body. _____

7. A session with the same (or about the same) open and close.
   _____

8. Thin lines above and below the candlestick's real body.
   _____

9. In a downtrend, a large, white real body which engulfs a small, black real body. _____

10. In a downtrend, a small real body at the top of a session's range with little or no upper shadow and a very long lower shadow.
    _____

## Problems

*NOTE: The figure numbers in parentheses are the corresponding text figures that can be referenced to check answers.*

**1.** Label the open, high, low, and close of these candles.

Figure 13.1                           Figure 13.2
BLACK REAL BODY            WHITE REAL BODY

**2.** Identify the following candlestick patterns.

Figure 13.5                                    Figure 13.7

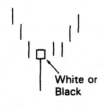                    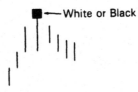

Figure 13.9                                    Figure 13.11

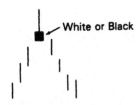                    

Figure 13.12

Figure 13.15

Figure 13.17

Figure 13.18

**3.** Draw the horizontal lines that define the rising window.

Figure 13.20

**4.** Draw the horizontal lines that define the falling window.
Figure 13.21

# 14
# Real-World Chart Analysis

Chapter 14, Real-World Chart Analysis, in *Technical Analysis*, displays 105 futures charts with Jack Schwager's reasons for entering and exiting trades. Because this chapter was designed as a hands-on chart-analysis experience in the main text, we will not duplicate that activity in this study guide. Instead, we have prepared a series of true/false questions that we hope will stimulate your thinking and serve as a review of the chapter.

## Questions - True or False

1. A flag formed near the top of a trading range is usually a bullish pattern.

   T    F

2. The ability of a market to move sideways near major resistance rather than pulling back reflects serious underlying weakness.

   T    F

3. It is often a good idea to move a stop closer to current prices when a market has reached a measured-move objective.

   T    F

4. A market is never too high to buy or too low to sell if there are good reasons to enter a trade and if the risk can be defined by a relatively close stop.

   T    F

5. A pullback to major support after a breakout from a continuation pattern would usually make a poor entry point for a long posi tion.

   T    F

6. When the primary premise for a trade is violated, a trader should not automatically liquidate his position.

   T    F

7. In every trade there is a tradeoff between the possibility of get- ting a better entry price and assuring that the position is imple mented.

   T    F

8. Never liquidate a trade just because the short-term price action suggests a possible reversal.

   T    F

**9.** A trader in a long position should usually not raise his stop higher than the nearest meaningful chart point.

T    F

**10.** A flag formed above an extended trading range often provides an excellent sell signal.

T    F

**11.** Wide-ranging days that close dramatically counter to a prior trend often provide strong evidence for a continuation of the prior trend.

T    F

**12.** A market's consolidation in a sideways pattern following a downswing usually leads to another downswing.

T    F

**13.** Chart analysis is a game of percentages, not absolutes.

T    F

**14.** A losing trade is the same as a trading mistake.

T    F

**15.** Confirmed bull-traps are among the most reliable chart signals for a major bottom.

T    F

**16.** Waiting for a trade to line up so that there are no major contradictory signals from the methodology being used will result in no trades ever being implemented.

T    F

**17.** Using flag and pennant consolidations as signals for trade entry and exit often makes it possible to keep losses small even when the pattern proves wrong.

T    F

**18.** Keeping losses small is probably more important to ultimate trading success than possessing a superior skill in picking trades.

T     F

**19.** Successful chart analysis is more a matter of accurately forecasting market direction than correctly responding to market price action.

T     F

**20.** A chart pattern does not have to be right more than 50% of the time to be valuable.

T     F

**21.** Flexibility in being able to change one's opinion may be the most important trait in the successful application of chart analysis to trading.

T     F

**22.** A flag consolidation formed in new high ground usually leads to at least a short-term downswing.

T     F

**23.** Multiple, simultaneous indicators can increase the reliability of a signal.

T     F

**24.** Additions to major position trades should be implemented regardless of the closeness of the nearest technically significant chart point.

T     F

**25.** It is not always necessary to wait for substantive proof of a top (or bottom) being in place before taking a trade based on the assumption that the trend has reversed.

T     F

**26.** You can't win in trading without being willing to lose.

T     F

**27.** After liquidating a position because a profit-target has been reached, a trader must avoid reentering the trade.

T    F

**28.** Taking profits without evidence of a reversal is a reasonable strategy if the open profit is large, has been realized quickly, and a major objective has been achieved.

T    F

**29.** A substantial portion of all trades—even those that look most promising—will turn out to be losers.

T    F

**30.** Placing stops too close can actually increase risk rather than decrease risk.

T    F

**31.** Using short-term chart patterns for timing the entry and exit of trades will always result in losses in wide-ranging trading-range markets.

T    F

**32.** Even if the chart picture changes dramatically, a position should not be liquidated on the same day that it was initiated.

T    F

**33.** Trading success depends less on correctly differentiating winners from losers in the trade-selection process and more on keeping the loss on losing trades much smaller than the gains on winning trades.

T    F

**34.** If a methodology that has proven itself profitable over the long run yields several consecutive losses, the trader must eliminate that methodology from his trading strategy.

T    F

**35.** Entering a trade counter to the direction of the short-term trend can be acceptable if the trade is in the direction of the long-term trend.

T    F

# 15
# Oscillators

An oscillator is a mathematically derived measure of a market's momentum. Momentum is defined as the rate of acceleration or deceleration of price changes. A declining oscillator in a rising market or a rising oscillator in a falling market indicates that the rate of price change in the direction of the trend is decreasing. An oscillator's failure to continue rising in an uptrend or falling in a downtrend can be interpreted as an early warning sign of a possible trend reversal.

Overbought and oversold levels are drawn through the oscillator's highest peaks and lowest valleys. To be most useful, an oscillator should be in overbought or oversold territory only about ten percent of the time. An overbought oscillator suggests that a market may have risen too far too fast, and an oversold oscillator warns that a market may have fallen farther and faster than usual.

Divergence is another important feature of oscillators. Bullish divergence occurs when an oscillator fails to make a new high along with a new price high;bearish divergence occurs when an oscillator fails to reach a new low when prices fall to a new low. Divergence can be viewed as another early warning sign of a possible change in trend.

Popular oscillators include the DMA oscillator, momentum, rate-of-change, MACD, RSI, and stochastic. The DMA oscillator measures the difference between a fast and a slow moving average to determine the momentum of the trend. The momentum oscillator is the difference between today's closing price and the close a specified number of days in the past. Rate-of-change is calculated by dividing today's closing price by the close of a selected number of days in the past. The MACD consists of two lines that are derived from three exponential moving averages. The MACD line is the difference between two EMAs, and the signal line is an EMA of the MACD line. RSI compares the relative strength of price gains on days that close above the previous day's close to price losses on days that close below the previous day's close. The stochastic oscillator measures market momentum by determining the relative position of closing prices within the high-low range of a specified number of days.

Oscillators perform well when a market is trading sideways but work poorly when a market is in a strong uptrend or downtrend. The reliability of oscillator signals can be improved with confirming indicators which include trendlines, moving averages, reversal days, the moving-average channel, and Micro-M tops/Micro-W bottoms.

## Questions - Multiple Choice

**1.** Using an MACD oscillator, a basic buy signal occurs when the MACD line _____ the signal line.

a.  crosses below

b.  equals

c.  crosses above

d.  parallels

**2.** A _____ occurs when a market makes a new high, declines, and rallies to a higher high, while an oscillator makes a high along with the market, declines, and then fails to make a new high.

a.  bullish divergence

b.  bearish divergence

c.  bullish convergence

d.  bearish convergence

**3.** After entering a long position using a combination of an oscillator's bullish divergence and the penetration of the moving-average channel, a stop loss could be set _____.

a.  above the moving average of highs

b.  below the moving average of highs

c.  above the moving average of lows

d.  below the moving average of lows

**4.** An oscillator should be in overbought or oversold territory only about _____ percent of the time.

a.  five

b.  ten

c.  twelve

d.  fifteen

**5.** If a dual moving-average oscillator is below zero and falling, the _____ is gaining _____ momentum.

a. uptrend, bullish

b. uptrend, bearish

c. downtrend, bullish

d. downtrend, bearish

**6.** After the up-day/down-day sequence in a Micro-W bottom, buy when prices rally above _____.

a. the high of the down-close/up-close pattern

b. the low of the up-day/down-day pattern

c. the high of the up-day/down-day pattern

d. the bullish divergence

**7.** Oscillators perform better in _____ markets.

a. nontrending

b. downtrending

c. uptrending

d. fast

**8.** The _____ oscillator is calculated by subtracting the closing price of N days ago from today's closing price.

a. dual moving-average

b. momentum

c. rate-of-change

d. stochastic

**9.** A _____ is a good measure of recent volatility.

a. Micro-W bottom

b. bullish divergence

c. bearish divergence

d. moving-average channel

**10.** The first step in the development of a Micro-M top is a
_____.

a. bearish-divergence high
b. bullish-divergence high
c. bearish-divergence low
d. bullish-divergence low

## Problems

*NOTE: The figure numbers in parentheses are the corresponding text figures that can be referenced to check answers.*

**1.** Label the overbought, oversold, and zero lines of the DMA oscillator.

Figure 15.2

OVERBOUGHT AND OVERSOLD LEVELS

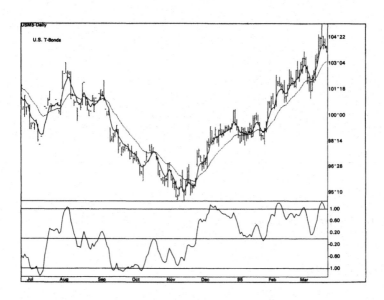

**2.** Identify the bullish divergence.

Figure 15.3

BULLISH DIVERGENCE

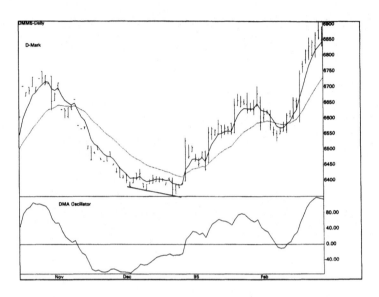

**3.** Identify the bearish divergence.

Figure 15.4

BEARISH DIVERGENCE

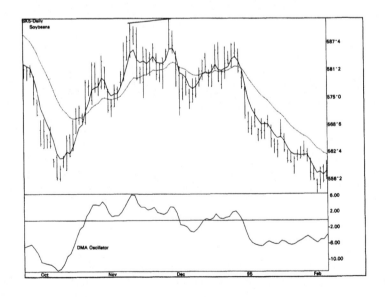

**4.** Identify the bearish divergence, draw the trendline that begins at the December low, and mark the trendline penetration that con firms the oscillator sell signal.

Figure 15.5

TREND LINE PENETRATION AS CONFIRMATION

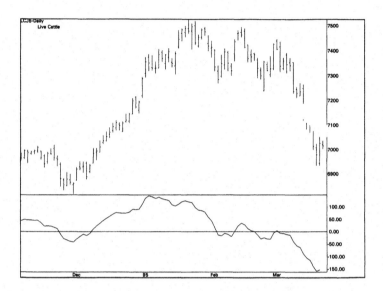

**5.** Identify the bullish divergence and mark the penetration of the moving average that confirms the oscillator buy signal.

Figure 15.6

EMA PENETRATION AS CONFIRMATION

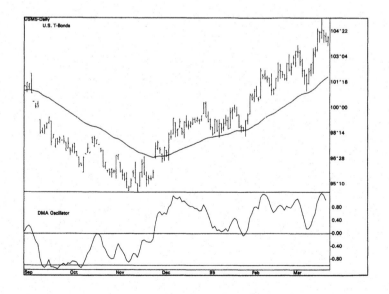

**6.** Identify the bullish divergence in December, the reversal day, the trendline break, and the penetration of the moving average.

Figure 15.15

CONFIRMATION OF BULLISH DIVERGENCE IN RSI

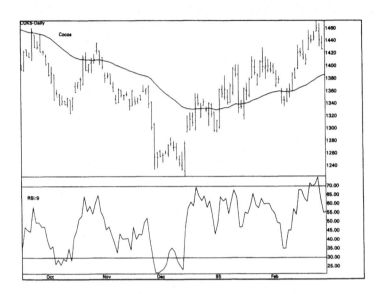

**7.** Identify the bearish divergence in January, the reversal day, the trendline break, and the penetration of the moving average.

Figure 15.16

CONFIRMATION OF BEARISH DIVERGENCE IN RSI

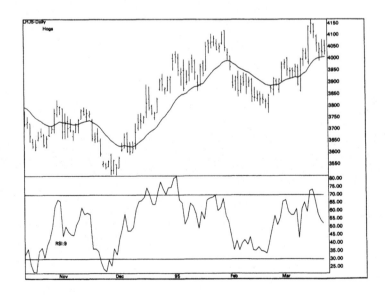

**8.** Identify the bullish divergence in February and mark the penetration of the moving-average channel that confirms the oscillator buy signal. Indicate where you would set your initial stop loss.

Figure15.20

UPSIDE PENETRATION OF MAC AS A BUY CONFIRMATION

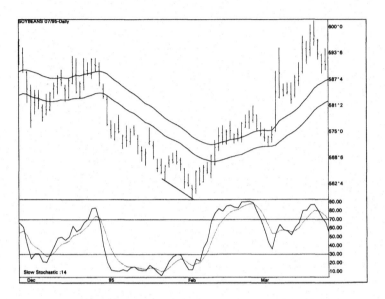

**9.** Identify the bullish divergence and label the four legs of the Micro-W bottom (a - d).

Figure 15.22

MICRO-W BOTTOM

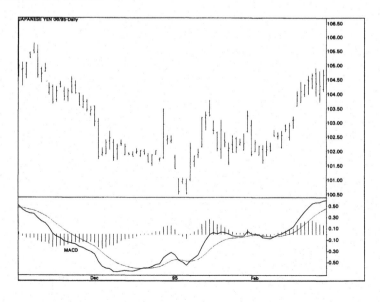

**10.** Identify the bearish divergence and label the Micro-M top (a - c).
Figure 15.23
MICRO-M TOP

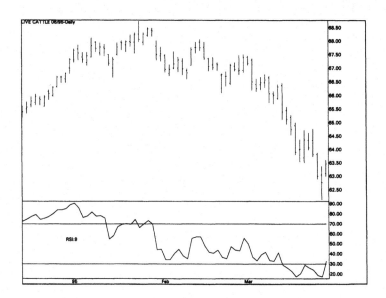

# 16
# Cycle Analysis of the Futures Market

Statistical analysis for the existence of cycles in many economic series is very strong. Cycles exist in market price data because cycles reflect lags that affect shifts in supply and demand and also reflect the psychological responses of traders to price swings. A data series consists of three components: growth forces, periodic forces, and random forces. Cycle analysis attempts to find periodic or recurring patterns in the data. The time span of a cycle from crest to crest or trough to trough is called its period. Frequency refers to the number of occurrences of a cycle in a given span of data. The phase of a cycle is the position in time of a center point of a wave. Amplitude is the strength of the fluctuation, and axis refers to the straight line around which a cycle fluctuates.

To make a complete cycle analysis of a data series, the technician must perform eight steps: (1) choose the data, (2) visually inspect the data, (3) transform data into log form, (4) smooth the data, (5) find possible cycles, (6) complete detrending of data by using departures from a moving average, (7) test the cycles for statistical significance and dominance, and (8) combine and project cycles into the future.

Traders who attempt to use cycles as a trading tool will encounter two basic problems: (1) market swings are not symmetrical, and (2) cycle tops and bottoms can be early or late. Cycle transition adjustments and cycle windows are attempts to reduce these problems. Although cycle analysis can be a useful tool for determining both market direction and timing, traders should remember that cycles are only one of many market forces and that even very consistent cycles will deviate from their mathematical representation. Cycles should never be relied on as the sole source of trading decisions.

## Questions - Multiple Choice

**1.** _____ data is best for analyzing cycles.

a.  Intraday

b.  Daily

c.  Weekly

d.  Quarterly

**2.** If a cycle is fourteen data points in length and the phase is five, then a crest occurs at the _____ data point.

a.  ninth

b.  tenth

c.  fourteenth

d.  nineteenth

**3.** Smoothing to eliminate or dampen random fluctuations is accomplished by taking a _____ moving average of the data.

a.  long-term centered

b.  long-term ending

c.  short-term centered

d.  short-term ending

**4.** _____ is commonly used to identify possible cycles.

a.  Harmonic analysis

b.  A Bartels test

c.  A histogram

d.  Spectral analysis

**5.** It is recommended that no more than _____ data points be used in cycle analysis.

a.  200

b.  1,000

c.  2,000

d.  5,000

**6.** The time span from crest to crest of a cycle is called its
_____.

a. frequency
b. period
c. amplitude
d. phase

**7.** Which of the following tests is not commonly used in cycle analysis? _____

a. Student's t
b. F-ratio
c. Chi-Square
d. Bartels

**8.** It is necessary to find the lengths of the potential cycles before completing the detrending process because the length of the moving average used in the departure series should be _____ the length of the cycle.

a. greater than
b. less than
c. equal to
d. at least twice

**9.** The _____ test measures both the amplitude and the phase of a cycle.

a. Student's t
b. F-ratio
c. Chi-Square
d. Bartels

**10.** Transforming data into _____ form normalizes percentage price swings.

a. moving-average
b. logarithmic

c.  periodic

d.  averaged

## Questions - Matching

Items:

(a) growth forces, (b) random forces, (c) frequency, (d) amplitude, (e) phase, (f) axis, (g) periodogram, (h) Fourier series, (i) spectral analysis, (j) Bartels test

**1.**  The length and depth of the wave above and below its axis.
_____

**2.**  Influences that cause time series to increase or decrease slowly over time. _____

**3.**  The position in time of a certain point of a wave. _____

**4.**  A cycle-analysis test that seeks to identify cycles by analyzing the data in tabular form. _____

**5.**  The number of occurrences of a cycle in a given span of data.
_____

**6.**  A measurement of the goodness of fit between the price series and the harmonic curve derived for the given cycle length being tested. _____

**7.**  An analysis routine that measures the strength of a cycle at each give frequency. _____

**8.**  Factors that cause irregular, unpredictable fluctuations in the data. _____

**9.**  An equation consisting of sines and cosines for filtering waves or cycles. _____

**10.**  The straight line around which a cycle fluctuates. _____

## Problems

*NOTE: The figure numbers in parentheses are the corresponding text figures that can be referenced to check answers.*

1.  In this illustration of the key components of data, label the lines that represent growth forces, periodic forces, and random forces.

Figure 16.4

KEY COMPONENTS OF DATA

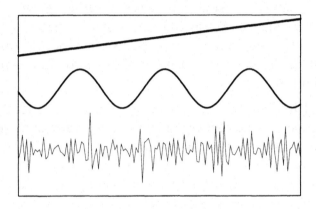

2.  In this ideal cycle model, label the following items: crest, trough, axis, period, phase, and amplitude.

Figure 16.5

IDEAL CYCLE MODEL

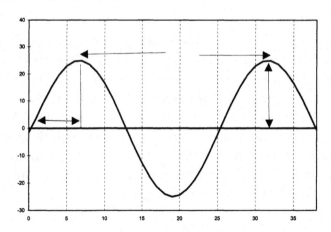

# 17

# Technical Trading Systems: Structure and Design

Five areas of system structure and design are discussed in this chapter: (1) basic trend-following systems, (2) key weaknesses of these systems, (3) guidelines for improving systems, (4) counter-trend systems, and (5) diversification. The benefits of trading with a mechanical system include eliminating emotion from trading, ensuring a consistency of approach, and providing a method for controlling risk.

The two basic types of trend-following systems are moving-average systems and breakout systems. The crossover moving-average approach generates a buy signal when a shorter moving average crosses above a longer moving average and a sell signal when a shorter moving average crosses below a longer moving average. Breakout systems are based on the idea that the ability of a market to move to a new high or new low indicates the potential for a continuation in the direction of the breakout. An example of a simple breakout system would be covering a short position and going long if today's close exceeds the prior N-day high and covering a long position and going short if today's close is below the prior N-day low. The value chosen for N determines the sensitivity of the system. Fast systems provide earlier signals but generate more false signals than slow systems do; the loss per trade in a slower system will be greater than the loss for the corresponding trade in a faster system. In most markets, slow systems tend to yield better results.

Although even basic moving-average or breakout systems generally prove profitable if traded consistently over many markets for an adequate length of time, simple trend-following systems normally expose the trader to large drawdowns. Traders can modify basic trend-following systems by requiring additional conditions to be met before signals are acted upon. Valid signals will fulfill the confirmation conditions, while false signals usually will not. Examples of confirming conditions include a minimum penetration, a time delay, and a specified pattern. Confirmation conditions reduce whipsaw losses but delay entry on valid signals.

Filters attempt to eliminate trades that have a below-average probability of success. In developing a filter, the system designer tries to find a common denominator applicable to the majority of losing trades. Systems can include both a filter and a confirmation rule. Only signals that pass the filter's requirement and that are later validated by the confirmation rule will result in actual trades.

Since bull and bear markets behave differently, with price declines from major tops tending to be more rapid than price rallies from major bottoms, it may be wise to use conditions for sell signals that are more sensitive than conditions used to generate buy signals. It is also desirable to develop an approach that allows for pyramiding, i.e. adding units to a base position in a major trend. Simple trend-following systems can usually be improved by using a trade exit rule that allows for the liquidation of a position prior to receiving a signal to enter a trade in the opposite direction.

Counter-trend systems attempt to achieve the difficult goal of buying low and selling high. Approaches that can be used to construct a counter-trend system include fading a minimum move, fading a minimum move with confirmation delay, oscillators, cycles, and contrary opinion.

Diversification can be achieved by trading across a broad range of markets, by trading each market with several systems, and by using different variations of each system. Three important benefits to diversification are: (1) dampened equity retracements, (2) ensured participation in major trends, and (3) bad-luck insurance.

## Questions - Multiple Choice

**1.** _____ is/are designed to reduce the number of false signals.
a. Moving averages
b. Diversification
c. Confirmation rules
d. Pyramiding

**2.** One of the main advantages of using a technical trading system is to eliminate _____ from trading decisions.
a. risk
b. emotion
c. losses
d. work

**3.** Overbought/oversold oscillator signals are an example of a _____ system.
a. pattern-recognition
b. trend-following
c. cyclic
d. counter-trend

**4.** A possible improvement to a system that surrenders a large percentage of open profits is to _____.
a. diversify
b. use exit rules
c. use confirmation rules
d. pyramid

**5.** It is essential to include _____ in a counter-trend system.
a. stop-loss conditions
b. breakout points
c. confirmation rules
d. penetration rules

**6.** In general, _____ conditions might be appropriate for generating sell signals.

a. less sensitive

b. more sensitive

c. less trending

d. more trending

**7.** Which two of the following are generally true of slow trend-following systems versus fast trend-following systems? _____ and _____

a. more transaction costs

b. more losing trades

c. lower transaction costs

d. fewer losing trades

**8.** A market moving to a new high or low serves as the basis of a(n) _____ system.

a. oscillator counter-trend

b. pattern-recognition

c. moving-average trend-following

d. breakout trend-following

**9.** A(n) _____ is applied at the same time the basic system signal is generated.

a. filter

b. pyramid

c. oscillator

d. confirmation rule

**10.** A key component of a mechanical trading system is _____.

a. the trader's advanced degree in economics

b. sound money management

c. the trader's intuition

d. a mainframe computer

# 18
# Examples of Original Trading Systems

In Chapter 18, Jack Schwager presents three original trading systems based on chart patterns that were introduced in Chapter 6. The systems are explained for the primary purpose of providing the reader with a sense of how technical concepts can be used in the development of a mechanical trading approach.

The wide-ranging day system defines trading ranges based on days that have a much wider true range than witnessed in recent trading sessions. Although the trading range can be defined as the wide-ranging day itself, the system can expand the trading range to encompass all the true highs and true lows during the period from N1 days before the wide-ranging day to N2 days after the wide-ranging day.

The run-day breakout system generates a buy signal when the market closes above the highest true high of a specified number of down-run days. Sell signals are generated when the market closes below the lowest true low of a specified number of up-run days. The logic behind the system is that a trend reversal is likely to have occurred when the market demonstrates the ability to close opposite the extreme point of one or more strongly trending days. The run-day consecutive count system is similar to the run-day breakout system, but it adds the requirement that the specified up-run days not be interrupted by any down-run days or that the specified number of down-run days not be interrupted by any up-run days. Although the systems presented can be traded as described, their main purpose is to illustrate the development of trading systems from basic chart patterns.

## Questions - Multiple Choice

**1.** The true high is the maximum of the current day's _____ and the previous day's _____.

a. close, close

b. close, high

c. high, close

d. high, high

**2.** In the run-day consecutive count system, a _____ count is begun when a sell signal is received.

a. sell

b. buy

c. trend

d. volatility

**3.** A volatility ratio parameter must be specified in the _____ system.

a. wide-ranging day

b. run-day breakout

c. run-day consecutive count

d. wide-ranging consecutive count

**4.** For the wide-ranging day system, N1 and N2 equal to _____ will result in a less favorable entry level (but fewer false signals).

a. zero

b. one

c. two

d. four

**5.** The _____ usually determine(s) the sensitivity of a trading system.

a. value of the parameters

b. trading signals

c. market

d. volatility ratio

## Questions - Matching

Items:

(a) wide-ranging day, (b) true high, (c) true low, (d) price trigger range, (e) up-run day, (f) down-run day, (g) buy count, (h) sell count, (i) true range, (j) volatility ratio

1. The number of down-run days without any intervening up-run days. _____

2. The true high minus the true low. _____

3. The maximum of the current day's high and the previous day's close. _____

4. A day that witnesses a much wider true range than that of recent trading sessions. _____

5. Today's true range divided by the true range of the past N-day period. _____

6. Activated when a sell signal is received and increased by one whenever a new up-run day occurs. _____

7. In the wide-ranging day system, the range defined by the highest true high and lowest true low in the interval between N1 days before the most recent wide-ranging day to N2 days after the wide-ranging day. _____

8. The minimum of the current day's low and the previous day's close. _____

9. A day with a true low less than the minimum true low of the past N days and a true high greater than the maximum true high of the subsequent N days. _____

**10.** A day with a true high greater than the maximum true high of the past N days and a true low less than the minimum true low of the subsequent N days. _____

# 19
# Selecting the Best Futures Price Series for Computer Testing

Testing trading systems on futures prices presents a problem because of the expiring contract characteristic of futures contracts. Four types of price series can be used to test trading systems: actual contract, nearest futures, constant-forward, and continuous. An actual contract series requires using a great number of individual contract price series and deciding how to treat rollover points from one contract to another contract. A nearest futures price series is a linked series that is constructed by taking each individual contract series until its expiration and then continuing with the next contract until its expiration, and so on. The problem with the nearest futures price series is that the price gaps between expiring and new contracts make it inappropriate for testing systems. A constant-forward (perpetual) price series consists of price quotes a constant amount of time forward, constructed from futures data using interpolation. Although the constant-forward series eliminates the price gaps at rollover points, it creates an untradable series and fails to reflect the evaporation of time that occurs in carrying-charge futures contracts. A continuous price series eliminates distortion due to rollover price gaps and precisely reflects the fluctuations of a futures position continuously rolled over. It is constructed by adjusting the forward contract on the rollover day by the difference between the forward and expiring contract on that date. That is, if the forward contract was trading at a premium, it would be adjusted downward by the premium on the rollover date. The adjustment continues until the current date is reached, and the final cumulative adjustment factor is added to all the continuous futures prices to translate the scale of the series to current levels.

## Questions - Multiple Choice

**1.** The major problem in using an actual individual contract series is the lack of _____ for much of the contract life.

a. price quotes

b. carrying charges

c. liquidity

d. options

**2.** The _____ price series would accurately reflect a constant long futures position.

a. actual-contract

b. nearest-futures

c. constant forward

d. continuous

**3.** In measuring the profits or losses of trades, a price series must accurately reflect _____.

a. price changes

b. price levels

c. percentage changes

d. carrying charges

**4.** For a continuous futures price series, the rollover price spreads (nearby-forward) are -2.80, -3.35, -3.94, and -1.75. The current price is 245.89. The unadjusted current continuous price is _____.

a. 257.73

b. 245.89

c. 244.14

d. 234.05

**5.** A constant-forward price series uses _____ to link futures contracts.

a. regression
b. interpolation
c. a simple average
d. a moving average

**6.** Use the following soybean futures price series to develop a continuous spread-adjusted price series.

a. What is the continuous price (after adjustment) for the August 93 contract on July 1, 1993?

b. What is the continuous price (after adjustment) for the March 95 contract on January 4, 1995?

| Date | Contract | Price |
| --- | --- | --- |
| 1/2/92 | Jan | 549.50 |
| 1/2/92 | Mar | 550.25 |
| 3/2/92 | Mar | 583.50 |
| 3/2/92 | May | 592.00 |
| 5/1/92 | May | 583.75 |
| 5/1/92 | July | 590.25 |
| 7/1/92 | July | 597.50 |
| 7/1/92 | Aug | 602.25 |
| 8/3/92 | Aug | 558.25 |
| 8/3/92 | Sept | 555.75 |
| 9/1/92 | Sept | 552.25 |
| 9/1/92 | Nov | 545.25 |
| 11/3/92 | Nov | 554.75 |
| 11/3/92 | Jan | 557.25 |
| 1/4/93 | Jan | 562.50 |
| 1/4/93 | Mar | 568.00 |

| | | |
|---------|------|--------|
| 3/1/93 | Mar | 581.25 |
| 3/1/93 | May | 584.25 |
| 5/3/93 | May | 591.75 |
| 5/3/93 | July | 594.00 |
| 7/1/93 | July | 658.25 |
| 7/1/93 | Aug | 659.75 |
| 8/2/93 | Aug | 704.50 |
| 8/2/93 | Sept | 705.50 |
| 9/1/93 | Sept | 652.50 |
| 9/1/93 | Nov | 654.75 |
| 11/1/93 | Nov | 618.50 |
| 11/1/93 | Jan | 628.50 |
| 1/3/94 | Jan | 698.75 |
| 1/3/94 | Mar | 709.00 |
| 3/1/94 | Mar | 678.50 |
| 3/1/94 | May | 684.50 |
| 5/2/94 | May | 669.75 |
| 5/2/94 | July | 669.75 |
| 7/4/94 | July | 643.00 |
| 7/4/94 | Aug | 639.75 |
| 8/1/94 | Aug | 585.00 |
| 8/1/94 | Sept | 571.50 |
| 9/1/94 | Sept | 580.75 |
| 9/1/94 | Nov | 574.00 |
| 11/1/94 | Nov | 542.25 |
| 11/1/94 | Jan | 554.25 |
| 1/4/95 | Jan | 548.50 |
| 1/4/95 | Mar | 558.50 |
| 3/1/95 | Mar | 553.75 |
| 3/1/95 | May | 563.50 |
| 3/22/95 | May | 580.00 |

# 20
# Testing and Optimizing Trading Systems

A trading system is a set of rules used to generate trade signals. A parameter is a value that can be freely assigned to vary the timing of signals. While "generic" systems are limited to one or two parameters, more complex systems will usually require three or more parameters. Generally, it is best to use the form of a system with the fewest parameters possible without incurring a significant deterioration in performance relative to the more complex forms of the system.

There are four types of parameters. Continuous parameters can assume any value within a given range. Discrete parameters can assume only integer values. Code parameters are used to represent definitional classifications. Fixed, nonoptimized parameters can help the system developer to avoid an excessive number of parameter sets.

A continuous futures series is the preferred choice for testing a system. The longer the test period, the more reliable the results. To determine the degree of time stability in a system, the developer should test the system over the period as a whole and then examine the results over various shorter time intervals. Due to faulty assumptions regarding transaction costs and limit days, a system's actual performance is often not as good as the simulated results would imply.

Optimization is the process of finding the best parameter set or sets for a particular system in a specified market with the assumption that the best parameter sets of the past will continue to provide superior results in the future. However, testing has revealed little if any correlation between past and future performance of optimized parameter sets.

Optimization can be somewhat more useful when applied to a portfolio of markets as opposed to being applied market-by-market. Instead of selecting the best past parameter set for each market, the system developer selects the best past single parameter set applied across all markets. The four factors that should be included in performance comparisons are: (1) percent return, (2) risk measure, (3) parameter stability, and (4) time stability.

Schwager presents five key conclusions regarding optimization: (1) any system can be made very profitable over its past performance through optimization, (2) optimization always overstates the potential future performance of a system, (3) generally, optimization will improve future performance of a system only marginally, if at all, (4) optimization may be of some value in defining the broad boundaries for the ranges from which parameters in a system should be chosen, and (5) sophisticated, complex optimization procedures are a waste of time.

Evaluating a system based on optimized parameter sets can be described as fitting the system to past results rather than actually testing the system. Two better approaches for evaluating a system are blind simulation and average parameter-set performance. Blind simulation optimizes data for a time period that excludes the most recent years; then the system is tested using the selected parameter sets for the subsequent years. Average parameter-set performance requires listing all parameter sets to test, running simulations for all the parameter sets selected, and then using the averages of all the sets tested as an indication of the system's performance.

The use of optimized results greatly distorts a system's implied future performance because there is very little, if any, correlation between the best-performing parameters for one period and the best performers for subsequent periods. The extraordinary misuse of simulations over many years has made simulated results virtually worthless. Schwager's corollary to Gresham's law of money states that "bad simulations drive out good simulations" (bad refers to simulations based on faulty assumptions).

A good system should demonstrate profitability in a large majority of actively traded markets. An important consideration in the selection of a system for trading a specific market is its performance over a broad range of markets. Another important aspect of testing trading systems is the potential value of negative results. When a system works well in most markets and for most parameter sets, but performs poorly in isolated cases, the system developer can analyze the conditions under which the system performs poorly to find previously overlooked weaknesses in the system. After detailing twelve steps in constructing and testing a trading system, Schwager concludes that designing a system with a truly superior performance is much more difficult than most people think.

## Questions - Multiple Choice

**1.** _____ is the difference between the assumed entry or exit level and the actual entry or exit level.

a.  Percent return

b.  Transaction cost

c.  Opportunity cost

d.  Slippage

**2.** The premise underlying optimization of trading systems is _____.

a.  superior-performing past parameter sets will maintain superiority in the future

b.  complexity is correlated with profitability

c.  every possible parameter value must be tested

d.  optimization results in perfect systems

**3.** Schwager's corollary to Gresham's law is _____.

a.  bad money drives out good money

b.  bad simulations drive out good simulations

c.  bad trading systems drive out good trading systems

d.  bad parameters drive out good parameters

**4.** Parameter stability and time stability are most closely related to _____.

a.  risk estimation

b.  completeness of data

c.  measuring volatility

d.  evaluating performance

**5.** The last step in constructing and testing a trading system is to compare results with _____ system results.

a.  generic

b.  optimized

c.  commercial

d.  fundamental

**6.** A backup stop rule used to prevent catastrophic losses would most likely be included in a trading-system test as a _____ parameter.

a.  continuous

b.  discrete

c.  code

d.  fixed

**7.** The appropriate price series for testing a system is generally a _____ series.

a.  continuous-futures

b.  nearest-futures

c.  constant-forward

d.  perpetual

**8.** All of the following should be considered in performance comparisons except _____.

a.  percent return

b.  risk measure

c.  the well-chosen example

d.  parameter stability

**9.** All of the following conclusions regarding optimization are true except _____.

a.  any system can be made to appear profitable through optimization

b.  optimization is not useful as a tool for defining the broad boundaries for the ranges from which parameter-set values should be chosen

c.  optimization overstates the potential future performance of a system

d.  for most systems, optimization will improve future performance only marginally, if at all

**10.** Which of these observations about trading systems is false? _____

a. in designing trend-following systems, one should concentrate on trying to discover a better method for defining trends rather than on modifications such as filters, confirmation rules, and stop rules

b. complexity is not necessarily a virtue

c. publicized simulated results are frequently optimized results

d. diversification can be extended to systems as well as to markets

## Questions - Matching

Items:

(a) trading system, (b) parameter, (c) continuous-futures series, (d) time stability, (e) parameter stability, (f) optimization, (g) suboptimal extreme ranges, (h) blind simulation, (i) average parameter-set performance, (j) negative results

**1.** The process of finding the best-performing parameter sets for a given system applied to a specific market. _____

**2.** Uses data that excludes the most recent years and then tests the system's performance using the selected parameter sets over subsequent years. _____

**3.** A set of rules that can be used to generate buy and sell signals. _____

**4.** The relative consistency of performance from one period to the next. _____

**5.** Requires defining a complete list of all parameter sets that one wishes to test before running any simulations. _____

**6.** Parameter sets that should be excluded from the selection of parameter-set values. _____

**7.** The preferred data series for testing a trading system. _____

**8.** Can reveal the conditions under which a system performs poorly and can provide clues for improving a system. _____

**9.** The degree to which similar parameter sets exhibit favorable performance. _____

**10.** A value assigned in a trading system to vary the timing of signals. _____

# 21
# Measuring Trading Performance

Rather than focusing exclusively on return when they evaluate money managers, investors should also include some measure of risk. The classic return-risk measure is the Sharpe Ratio which is a ratio of expected returns (sometimes adjusted by the risk-free interest rate) to the standard deviation of returns. If the standard deviation is low, one can assume that the actual return will be close to the expected return; if the standard deviation is high, there may be significant variance between the actual return and the expected return. The Sharpe Ratio can present a distorted picture due to its use of annualized average returns for the measure of gain, failure to distinguish between upside and downside fluctuations, and failure to distinguish between intermittent losses and consecutive losses.

Alternative risk/return measures include the Return Retracement Ratio (RRR), the Annual Gain to Pain Ratio (AGPR), and maximum loss. RRR addresses the distortions of the Sharpe Ratio by representing the ratio of the average annualized compounded return to an average annual maximum retracement measure. RRR comes closer than the Sharpe Ratio to defining risk in the way that most traders actually perceive risk. AGPR is the ratio of the arithmetic average of annual returns to the average annual maximum retracement. Although RRR is technically a better return/retracement measure than AGPR, some traders prefer AGPR because it is easier to compute and to understand. An AGPR of three, for example, means simply that the average annual return is three times as large as the average annual worst retracement. Additional important information can be obtained from maximum loss, the largest retracement experienced during the survey period if trading was initiated on the worst possible start date.

Two other performance measures, Expected Net Profit per Trade (ENPPT) and the Trade-Based Profit/Loss Ratio (TBPLR), should also be considered. ENPPT identifies systems that are susceptible to significant deterioration if transaction costs increase. TBPLR is the ratio of dollars gained to dollars lost in all trades.

The Sharpe Ratio and the superior return/risk measure RRR together can provide a very good description of a system's or a trader's relative performance. When evaluating money managers, the percent return and risk figures should be considered independently rather than exclusively as a ratio.

Net asset value and underwater curve are two types of charts that can be useful in comparing the performance of money managers. Net asset value refers to the equity at each specified point in time (usually at month-end) based on a $1,000 beginning equity. The underwater curve represents the percent drawdown at the end of each month, measured from the previous equity peak.

## Questions - Multiple Choice

1. Among the following, the _____ is considered the closest approximation of risk as perceived by traders.

a. standard deviation of returns

b. average annual maximum retracement

c. average maximum retracement

d. maximum loss

2. If a trader experiences a net loss in 55% of his total trades, an average net profit of $326, and an average net loss of $124, his expected net profit per trade is _____.

a. $215.10

b. $78.50

c. -$68.20

d. $146.70

3. In comparing trading performance, the _____ is the most widely used measure.

a. Sharpe Ratio

b. Return Retracement Ratio

c. Annual Gain to Pain Ratio

d. Trade-Based Profit/Loss Ratio

4. If a trader was worried about an increase in slippage, he would use the _____ to evaluate the impact of these increased costs.

a. Sharpe Ratio

b. Annual Gain to Pain Ratio

c. Trade-Based Profit/Loss Ratio

d. Expected Net Profit per Trade

**5.** A(n) _____ of two would mean that the average annual return is _____ times as large as the average annual worst retracement.

a. Sharpe Ratio, .5

b. Return Retracement Ratio, .5

c. Return Retracement Ratio, 2

d. Annual Gain to Pain Ratio, 2

**6.** The _____ reflects the maximum possible equity retracement at the end of each period.

a. standard deviation of equity

b. underwater curve

c. net asset value curve

d. average annualized compounded return

**7.** If a money manager experienced a -20% return in the first month, a -5% return in the second month, and a +30% return in the third month, the net asset value at the end of the third month is _____ (assuming a beginning equity of $1,000).

a. 1050

b. 1586

c. 988

d. 450

**8.** Using maximum loss as a measure of risk would introduce a bias in favor of traders with _____ trade records.

a. shorter

b. longer

c. higher-return

d. lower-return

**9.** The _____ return is the constant rate of return that, if compounded annually, would yield the enging equity give the starting equity.

a. average annual

b. annualized compounded

c.   annualized

d.   average

**10.** Traders are generally more concerned with _____ in equity rather than volatility in equity.

a.   percent return

b.   upside volatility

c.   annualized compounded return

d.   downside volatility

## Questions - Matching

Items:

(a) Sharpe Ratio, (b) standard deviation, (c) Return Retracement Ratio, (d) Annual Gain to Pain Ratio, (e) maximum loss, (f) Expected Net Profit per Trade, (g) Trade-Based Profit/Loss Ratio, (h) net asset value, (i) underwater curve, (j) return and risk

**1.**   The arithmetic average of annual returns divided by the average annual maximum retracement. _____

**2.**   The classic return-risk measure, based on standard deviations. _____

**3.**   A graphic depiction of the percent drawdown at month-end, measured from the previous equity peak. _____

**4.**   A chart of the equity at month-end based on a beginning equity of $1,000. _____

**5.**   A statistic that measures the degree of dispersion in the data. _____

**6.**   Identifies systems that are vulnerable to major deterioration due to increased transaction costs but does not include a risk measure. _____

**7.**   Should be evaluated independently rather than solely as a ratio. _____

**8.** Indicates the ratio of dollars gained to dollars lost in all trades. _____

**9.** Represents the average annualized compounded return divided by an average maximum retracement. _____

**10.** The largest retracement during the survey period if trading began on the worst possible start date. _____

# 22
# The Planned Trading Approach

Successful futures speculators maintain a systematic, disciplined approach to trading. A meaningful trading philosophy can be based on fundamental analysis, chart analysis, technical-trading systems, or a combination of these approaches. The trading strategy should be a specific as possible.

To select the markets to be traded, the speculator should consider the suitability to the trading approach, diversification, and volatility. A risk-control plan should include a restriction on the percentage of total funds allocated to any trade, a stop-loss strategy, diversification, reduced leverage for correlated markets, market-volatility adjustments, leverage-to-equity-change adjustments, and losing-period adjustments (for discretionary traders only).

A daily planning routine sets time aside each evening for updating trading systems and charts, planning new trades, and updating exit points for existing positions. A speculator should also take time to maintain a trading notebook and a diary and to analyze his past trades in order to identify the strengths and weaknesses of his approach and of his performance.

## Questions - Multiple Choice

**1.** Using _____ would be the most specific trading strategy.
a. fundamental analysis
b. a mechanical trading system
c. chart analysis
d. expert advice

**2.** The _____ is the most critical ingredient in successful trading.
a. optimization of a system
b. type of analysis used
c. choice of broker
d. control of losses

**3.** Specifying the maximum risk per trade is most closely related to _____.
a. a trading philosophy
b. a risk-control plan
c. a trader's notebook
d. fundamental analysis

**4.** A trader's _____ would include stop points, objectives, and risk exposure on open positions.
a. portfolio
b. diary
c. notebook
d. equity chart

**5.** A trader's diary can help a trader discover _____.
a. market secrets
b. personal strengths and weaknesses
c. entry points
d. trailing stops

**6.** A trader with limited funds should _____ extremely volatile markets.

a. leverage

b. pyramid

c. daytrade

d. avoid

**7.** The major problem of most futures traders is a lack of _____.

a. discipline

b. money

c. insider information

d. market information

**8.** Factors that should be considered in selecting markets to trade include all of the following except _____.

a. suitability to trading approach

b. diversification

c. optimization

d. volatility

**9.** The main elements of a risk-control plan include all of the following except _____.

a. maximum risk per trade

b. contrary opinion

c. market-volatility adjustments

d. a stop-loss strategy

**10.** Which of the following is not a true statement about defining a trading philosophy? _____

a. getting a trade idea from reading the newspaper is an example of an organized trading plan

b. the more specific the trading strategy the better

c.  a meaningful strategy can be based on fundamentals, charts, technical-trading systems, or a combination of these approaches

d.  the same method will not necessarily be used in all markets

# 23
# Eighty-Two Trading Rules and Market Observations

Although each speculator must discover his or her own trading truths, some trading guidelines can help to decrease the pain and increase the efficiency of the learning process. Schwager presents eighty-two suggestions related to entering and exiting trades, risk control and money management, holding and exiting winning trades, market patterns, and analysis of personal trading activity.

## Questions - Multiple Choice

**1.** Protective stop points should be determined _____.
a. after the trade has become profitable
b. after the trade has become unprofitable
c. by market reaction to your trading position
d. when the trade is entered

**2.** If a market sets new historical highs and holds, the odds favor a _____ move.
a. strong, bearish
b. strong, bullish
c. weak, bearish
d. weak, bullish

**3.** The failure of a market to follow through on significant bullish or bearish news is often an indication of a _____.
a. potential trend reversal
b. congestion pattern
c. spike
d. trend continuation

**4.** Most successful trades are the result of _____.
a. luck
b. intraday decisions
c. following expert advice
d. a trading plan

**5.** Winning trades tend to _____.
a. take time to develop
b. rebound from initial losses
c. generate gains from the start
d. be short-term in nature

**6.** The key to successful speculation is _____ .

a. limiting losses

b. forecasting market prices

c. developing trading systems

d. having a good broker

**7.** Two successive flags with little separation indicate a _____ pattern.

a. reversal

b. divergence

c. runaway

d. continuation

**8.** For a discretionary trader in a stretch of losing trades, it is sug-gested that position size be _____ , stop-loss points be _____ , and _____ new trades be initiated.

a. increased, tightened, more

b. decreased, tightened, fewer

c. decreased, loosened, fewer

d. increased, loosened, more

**9.** _____ are good short-term reversal signals.

a. Wide gaps

b. Flags

c. Pennants

d. Spikes

**10.** When a major report is about to be released, it is suggested that _____

a. large positions be entered

b. large positions be avoided

c. positions be reversed

d. positions be pyramided

## Questions - True or False

1. When you miss the first major portion of a new trend, it is usually best to refrain from taking any trades within that trend.

   T    F

2. Fading recent price-failure patterns is generally a poor choice.

   T    F

3. A reliable short-term trading strategy is to fade the first gap of a price move.

   T    F

4. Don't be hesitant to double your position on a retracement to the original entry point after having been ahead in a trade.

   T    F

5. Exit the trade if market action violates the trade's original premise even if the stop point has not been reached.

   T    F

6. Always pay more attention to objectives and support/resistance areas than to market action and evolving patterns.

   T    F

7. A failed signal is more reliable than the original signal.

   T    F

8. If a market suddenly witnesses a very great increase in volatility in the opposite direction of your position, exit the trade immediately.

   T    F

9. Narrow market consolidations near the upper boundary of wider trading ranges are reliable bearish patterns.

   T    F

**10.** Major tops and bottoms rarely occur without extreme sentiment readings.

T    F

# 24
# Market Wiz(ar)dom

Although successful traders employ a wide variety of methods, some general principles, especially psychological factors, are crucial for a profitable, long-term trading experience. Most of Schwager's observations in this chapter relate to an understanding of yourself and the market. It is more important to be able to read the market than to try to beat the market. Thus, many of the principles apply to personal goals, motivations, and discipline. The basic personal principle is to have a trading plan that is consistent with your own style and personality. The basic market principle is that prices exhibit nonrandom behavior that can be detected and exploited for profitable trading. A trading plan, discipline, money management, and diligent monitoring of personal performance are necessary conditions for successful trading.

## Questions - Multiple Choice

**1.** A trader should concentrate on maximizing _____.

a. the success rate of trades

b. the probability of a winning trade

c. entry levels

d. total gains from trading

**2.** Amateurs go broke by taking _____, while professionals go broke by taking _____.

a. large losses, small profits

b. large losses, large losses

c. small losses, large losses

d. small losses, small profits

**3.** The emotional state most desirable for successful trading is _____.

a. exhilaration

b. stress

c. fear

d. calmness

**4.** The best way to get an edge in trading is to _____.

a. purchase a trading system

b. develop your own method

c. listen to your broker

d. study the newspaper

**5.** Most highly successful traders consider _____ to be the most important factor.

a. luck

b. entry rules

c. money management

d. brokers

**6.** The easiest part of the trend to capture is the _____ portion.

a. middle
b. final
c. beginning
d. transitional

**7.** All of the following are necessary for profitable trading except _____.

a. an edge
b. money management
c. discipline
d. superior price-forecasting talent

**8.** Which of the following is not mentioned as a key element of trading success? _____

a. breaking down overwhelming goals into manageable chunks
b. finding a good source of inside information
c. keeping full concentration in the present moment
d. making self-to-self comparisons to measure progress

**9.** All of the following are important features of money management and risk control except _____.

a. not risking more than five percent of your capital on any trade
b. determining your exit point before getting into a trade
c. doubling up on your position when a trade moves against you
d. cutting trading size down during losing streaks

**10.** Which of the following is not a tenet of market wiz(ar)dom? _____

a. the urge to seek advice betrays a lack of confidence; think independently
b. a trading plan should reflect a personal core philosophy
c. if you have to win, you will wind.
d. whether you win or lose, you are responsible for your own trading results

# PART TWO

# Answers & Solutions

# 1
# Charts: Forecasting Tool or Folklore

**Answers - Multiple Choice**

1. c. statistical nature
2. d. patterns
3. b. nonrandom
4. a. discipline
5. c. trading with the trend
6. d. charts reveal basic behavioral patterns that can be used to anticipate major market trends
7. c. charts accurately forecast every market swing
8. b. markets seem to exhibit periods of nonrandom behavior

# 2
# Types of Charts

**Answers - Multiple Choice**

1.  b.  nearby futures
2.  c.  two X's
3.  a.  candlestick

**Answers - Matching**

1.  b.  point and figure chart
2.  e.  candlestick chart
3.  j.  close-only
4.  g.  shadows
5.  i.  continuous futures
6.  f.  real body
7.  d.  reversal size
8.  h.  nearest futures chart
9.  a.  daily bar chart
10. c.  box size

# 3
# Trends

## Answers - Multiple Choice

1.  d. arbitrary
2.  d. false
3.  b. TD
4.  a. buy
5.  b. one
6.  a. the high or the previous close, whichever is higher
7.  c. short
8.  a. rising
9.  d. larger, smaller
10. c. internal uptrend

## Solutions - Problems

The figure numbers in parentheses are the corresponding text numbers that should be referenced to check answers. See *Technical Analysis*, Chapter 3, figures 3.4, 3.7, 3.9, 3.10, 3.11, 3.13, 3.15, 3.16, 3.26, 3.34 for the solutions to problems 1-10.

# 4
# Trading Ranges

## Answers - Multiple Choice

1. b. false signal
2. c. longer
3. d. narrow, more
4. b. false signals
5. d. a lack of solid fundamental reasons to sustain the trend

## Solutions - Problems

The figure numbers in parentheses are the corresponding text numbers that should be referenced to check answers. See *Technical Analysis*, Chapter 4, figures 4.5, 4.7, 4.9 for the solutions to problems 1-3.

# 5
# Support and Resistance

## Answers - Multiple Choice

1. b. resistance
2. d. three-year
3. a. daily individual
4. c. Moving averages
5. a. 210,190

## Solutions - Problems

The figure numbers in parentheses are the corresponding text numbers that should be referenced to check answers. See *Technical Analysis*, Chapter 5, figures 5.2, 5.3, 5.15, 5.22 for the solutions to problems 1-4.

# 6
# Chart Patterns

## Answers - Multiple Choice

1. a. high, low
2. a. common
3. c. runaway
4. d. exhaustion
5. b. breakaway
6. c. a close near the high of the day's range
7. a. high
8. c. upthrust, downthrust
9. d. a downside trend reversal
10. a. V tops and bottoms
11. b. flags and pennants
12. a. parallel
13. c. bearish
14. c. the neckline is penetrated
15. d. island top

## Answers - Matching

1. i. descending triangle
2. e. down run day
3. k. double bottom
4. a. gap day
5. j. V top
6. c. reversal low day
7. g. symmetrical triangle
8. l. head-and-shoulders top
9. b. spike low

10. o. island reversal top

11. m. rounded bottom

12. f. wide-range day

13. n. rising wedge

14. d. upthrust day

15. h. ascending triangle

## Solutions - Problems

The figure numbers in parentheses are the corresponding text numbers that should be referenced to check answers. See *Technical Analysis,* Chapter 6, figures 6.2, 6.20, 6.23, 6.24, 6.28, 6.31, 6.35, 6.40, 6.41, 6.46, 6.47, 6.50, 6.53, 6.59, 6.63 for the solutions to problems 1-15.

# 7
# Is Chart Analysis Still Valid?

**Answers - Multiple Choice**

1.  a. losses are rigidly controlled and profitable trades are allowed to run their course
2.  c. tradeoff
3.  d. specific chart pattern
4.  c. a failed signal
5.  a. individualized

# 8
# Midtrend Entry and Pyramiding

## Answers - Multiple Choice

1.  c.  35 to 65%

2.  b.  reversal-of-minor-reaction

3.  c.  continuation-pattern

4.  b.  a daily price bar crossing a 40-day moving average from above

5.  a.  don't pyramid unless you can add the new contracts at a more favorable price lower than the last addition if long, higher than the last addition if short

## Solutions - Problems

The figure numbers in parentheses are the corresponding text numbers that should be referenced to check answers. See *Technical Analysis*, Chapter 8, figures 8.4, 8.5, 8.6 for the solutions to problems 1-3.

# 9
# Choosing Stop-Loss Points

## Answers - Multiple Choice

1. d. money management
2. b. below
3. c. money
4. d. trailing stop
5. a. reduce risk or protect profits

## Solutions - Problems

The figure numbers in parentheses are the corresponding text numbers that should be referenced to check answers. See *Technical Analysis*, Chapter 9, figures 9.1, 9.4 for the solutions to problems 1-2.

# 10
# Setting Objectives and Other Position Exit Criteria

## Answers - Multiple Choice

1. b. oversold
2. d. top of the head to the neckline
3. c. setup, buy
4. c. measured-move
5. b. sentiment
6. b. 665, 711, 805
7. a. 8, setup
8. d. long
9. c. chart-based
10. a. trailing-stop

## Solutions - Problems

The figure numbers in parentheses are the corresponding text numbers that should be referenced to check answers. See *Technical Analysis*, Chapter 10, figures 10.2, 10.16 for the solutions to problems 1-2.

# 11

# The Most Important Rule
# in Chart Analysis

## Answers - Multiple Choice

1. d. long
2. a. below, low
3. b. ignore, profit from
4. b. breakaway
5. d. false, conventional
6. d. close
7. b. bull, top
8. a. overbought/oversold confirmation
9. c. bullish
10. d. more popular

## Solutions - Problems

The figure numbers in parentheses are the corresponding text numbers that should be referenced to check answers. See *Technical Analysis*, Chapter 11, figures 11.1, 11.3, 11.7, 11.10, 11.16, 11.28, 11.30, 11.40 for the solutions to problems 1-8.

# 12
# Linking Contracts for Long-Term Chart Analysis: Nearest versus Continuous Futures

**Answers - Multiple Choice**

1. c. 11 cents
2. b. levels
3. c. major tops and bottoms
4. d. 63
5. b. a combination of nearest and continuous price series

# 13

# An Introduction to Japanese Candlestick Charts

## Answers - Multiple Choice

1. a. bearish
2. b. morning star
3. c. rising window
4. d. real body
5. b. bearish-continuation

## Answers - Matching

1. f. shooting star
2. i. evening star
3. a. real body
4. e. hanging man
5. j. window
6. h. dark cloud cover
7. c. doji
8. b. shadows
9. g. bullish engulfing pattern
10. d. hammer

## Solutions - Problems

The figure numbers in parentheses are the corresponding text numbers that should be referenced to check answers. See *Technical Analysis*, Chapter 13, figures 13.1, 13.2, 13.5, 13.7, 13.9, 13.11, 13.12, 13.15, 13.17, 13.18, 13.20, 13.21 for the solutions to problems 1-4.

# 14
# Real-World Chart Analysis

**Answers - True or False**

1.  T
2.  F
3.  T
4.  T
5.  F
6.  F
7.  T
8.  F
9.  T
10. F
11. F
12. T
13. T
14. F
15. F
16. F
17. T
18. T
19. F
20. T
21. T
22. F
23. T
24. F
25. T
26. T

27. F
28. T
29. T
30. T
31. F
32. F
33. T
34. F
35. T

# 15
# Oscillators

## Answers - Multiple Choice

1. c. crosses above
2. b. bearish divergence
3. d. below the moving average of lows
4. b. ten
5. d. downtrend, bearish
6. c. the high of the up-day/down-day pattern
7. a. nontrending
8. b. momentum
9. d. moving-average channel
10. a. bearish-divergence high

## Solutions - Problems

The figure numbers in parentheses are the corresponding text numbers that should be referenced to check answers. See *Technical Analysis*, Chapter 15, figures 15.2, 15.3, 15.5, 15.6, 15.15, 15.16, 15.20, 15.22, 15.23 for the solutions to problems 1-10.

# 16
# Cycle Analysis of the Futures Market

## Answers - Multiple Choice

1. b. daily
2. d. nineteenth
3. c. short-term centered
4. d. Spectral analysis
5. c. 2,000
6. b. period
7. a. Student's t
8. c. equal to
9. d. Bartels
10. b. logarithmic

## Answers - Matching

1. d. amplitude
2. a. growth forces
3. e. phase
4. g. periodogram
5. c. frequency
6. j. Bartels test
7. i. spectral analysis
8. b. random forces
9. h. Fourier series
10. f. axis

## Solutions - Problems

The figure numbers in parentheses are the corresponding text numbers that should be referenced to check answers. See *Technical Analysis*, Chapter 16, figures 16.4, 16.5 for the solutions to problems 1-2.

# 17
# Technical Trading Systems: Structure and Design

**Answers - Multiple Choice**

1. c. confirmation rules
2. b. emotion
3. d. counter-trend
4. b. use exit rules
5. a. stop-loss conditions
6. b. more sensitive
7. c.  lower transaction costs; and d. fewer losing trades
8. d. breakout trend-following
9. a. filter
10. b. sound money management

# 18
# Examples of Original Trading Systems

## Answers - Multiple Choice
1.  c.  high, close
2.  b.  buy
3.  a.  wide-ranging day
4.  d.  four
5.  a.  value of the parameters

## Answers - Matching
1.  h.  sell count
2.  i.  true range
3.  b.  true high
4.  a.  wide-ranging day
5.  j.  volatility ratio
6.  g.  buy count
7.  d.  price trigger range
8.  c.  true low
9.  f.  down-run day
10. e.  up-run day

# 19
# Selecting the Best Futures Price Series for Computer Testing

**Answers - Multiple Choice**

1.  c. liquidity
2.  d. continuous
3.  a. price changes
4.  d. 234.05
5.  b. interpolation
6.  a. 697.5.  The unadjusted continuous futures price is 634.

    b. 568.25.  The unadjusted continuous futures price is 504.75.

# 20

# Testing and Optimizing Trading Systems

## Answers - Multiple Choice

1. d. Slippage
2. a. superior-performing past parameter sets will maintain superiority in the future
3. b. bad simulations drive out good simulations
4. d. evaluating performance
5. a. generic
6. d. fixed
7. a. continuous-futures
8. c. the well-chosen example
9. b. optimization is not useful as a tool for defining the broad boundaries for the ranges from which parameter-set values should be chosen
10. a. in designing trend-following systems, one should concentrate on trying to discover a better method for defining trends rather than on modifications such as filters, confirmation rules, and stop rules

## Answers - Matching

1. f. optimization
2. h. blind simulation
3. a. trading system
4. d. time stability
5. i. average parameter-set performance
6. g. suboptimal extreme ranges
7. c. continuous-futures series
8. j. negative results
9. e. parameter stability
10. b. parameter

# 21
# Measuring Trading Performance

### Answers - Multiple Choice

1.  c.  average maximum retracement
2.  b.  $78.50
3.  a.  Sharpe Ratio
4.  d.  Expected Net Profit per Trade
5.  d.  Annual Gain to Pain Ratio, 2
6.  b.  underwater curve
7.  c.  988
8.  a.  shorter
9.  b.  annualized compounded
10. d.  downside volatility

### Answers - Matching

1.  d.  Average Gain to Pain Ratio
2.  a.  Sharpe Ratio
3.  i.  underwater curve
4.  h.  net asset value
5.  b.  standard deviation
6.  f.  Expected Net Profit per Trade
7.  j.  return and risk
8.  g.  Trade-Based Profit/Loss Ratio
9.  c.  Return Retracement Ratio
10. e.  maximum loss

# 22
# The Planned Trading Approach

**Answers - Multiple Choice**

1.  b.  a mechanical trading system
2.  d.  control of losses
3.  b.  a risk-control plan
4.  c.  notebook
5.  b.  personal strengths and weaknesses
6.  d.  avoid
7.  a.  discipline
8.  c.  optimization
9.  b.  contrary opinion
10. a.  getting a trade idea from reading the newspaper is an example of an organized trading plan

# 23
# Eighty-Two Trading Rules and Market Observations

## Answers - Multiple Choice

1. d. when the trade is entered
2. b. strong, bullish
3. a. potential trend reversal
4. d. a trading plan
5. c. generate gains from the start
6. a. limiting losses
7. d. continuation
8. b. decreased, tightened, fewer
9. d. Spikes
10. b. large positions be avoided

## Answers - True or False

1. F
2. T
3. F
4. F
5. T
6. F
7. T
8. T
9. F
10. T

# 24
# Market Wiz(ar)dom

**Answers - Multiple Choice**

1. d. total gains from trading
2. a. large losses, small profits
3. d. calmness
4. b. develop your own method
5. c. money management
6. a. middle
7. d. superior price-forecasting talent
8. b. finding a good source of inside information
9. c. doubling up on your position when a trade moves against you
10. c. if you have to win, you will win

# ABOUT THE AUTHORS

**Thomas A. Bierovic** is president of Synergy Futures and has been trading successfully since 1970. During the past five years, Tom has presented highly rated trading seminars in 32 countries on six continents. He also teaches several classes each year at the Chicago Board of Trade Commodities Institute, lectures at the annual Dow Jones/Telerate TAG Conference, and conducts private workshops for traders at his office in Wheaton, Illinois. Mr. Bierovic is the author of the trading manual *A Synergetic Approach to Profitable Trading*. He also contributed the chapter "Oscillators" to Jack Schwager's 1995 book *Schwager on Futures: Technical Analysis*. Tom is the instructor on Futures Learning Center's video series "Synergetic Technical Analysis" and an instructor on the Futures and Options Trading School video course. *Futures* magazine selected Tom for its Trader Profile in July, 1995, and *Futures World News* featured an interview with Tom in April, 1996. *Synergy Fax* (Tom's daily market letter) and "All-Star Traders Hotline" (a telephone advisory service) give specific recommendations for trading the U.S. futures markets. Tom is working on a new book about synergetic technical analysis for John Wiley & Sons.

**Dr. Steven C. Turner** is an Associate Professor of Agricultural and Applied Economics at the University of Georgia. He has taught courses on futures and options markets since 1987 and won teaching awards at the departmental, college, university, and national levels. In 1992, the American Agricultural Economics Association selected Dr. Turner as their Distinguished Undergraduate Teaching Award recipient. Dr. Turner has also published research results in the *Journal of Futures Markets, Review of Futures Markets, American Journal of Agricultural Economics, Agribusiness: An International Journal, Review of Agricultural Economics, and the Journal of Agricultural and Applied Economics.*

**Jack D. Schwager** is the CEO of Wizard Trading, a Commodity Trading Advisor firm that currently manages over $60 million. He was previously the Director of Futures Research for Prudential Securities, Inc. and has 22 years experience in heading up futures research departments. Mr. Schwager is the author of the highly regarded *A Complete Guide to the Futures*

**163**

*Markets, Technical Analysis, Fundamental Analysis,* and *Managed Trading,* published by John Wiley & Sons, Inc., and the best-selling *Market Wizards* and *New Market Wizards.* His writing has appeared in many publications, including *The New York Times* and *Forbes.* Much in demand as a speaker, he has lectured on a range of analytical topics, with a particular focus on great traders, technical analysis, and trading system development and evaluation.